EAT
YOURSELF
CALM

EAT
YOURSELF
CALM

INGREDIENTS & RECIPES
TO REDUCE THE STRESS IN YOUR LIFE

GILL PAUL
NUTRITIONIST: KAREN SULLIVAN, ASET, VTCT, BSC

hamlyn

An Hachette UK Company
www.hachette.co.uk

First published in Great Britain in 2014 by Hamlyn,
a division of Octopus Publishing Group Ltd
Endeavour House
189 Shaftesbury Avenue
London WC2H 8JY
www.octopusbooks.co.uk

Gill Paul asserts the moral right to be identified as
the author of this work.

ISBN 978-0-60062-747-0

A CIP catalogue record for this book
is available from the British Library

Printed and bound in China

10 9 8 7 6 5 4 3 2 1

All reasonable care has been taken in the
preparation of this book but the information
it contains is not intended to take the place of
treatment by a qualified medical practitioner.

People with known nut allergies should avoid
recipes containing nuts or nut derivatives,
and vulnerable people should avoid dishes
containing raw or lightly cooked eggs.

Both metric and imperial measurements have been
given in all recipes. Use one set of measurements
only, and not a mixture of both.

Standard level spoon and cup measurements
are used in all recipes

Ovens should be preheated to the specified
temperature – if using a fan-assisted oven,
follow the manufacturer's instructions for adjusting
the time and temperature.

Large eggs should be used unless
otherwise stated.

Some of the recipes in this book have previously
appeared in other titles published by Hamlyn.

Art Director: Jonathan Christie
**Photographic Art Direction, Prop Styling
and Design:** Isabel de Cordova
Photography: Will Heap
Food Styling: Joy Skipper
Editors: Katy Denny & Alex Stetter
Picture Library Manager: Jen Veall
Assistant Production Manager: Caroline Alberti

CONTENTS

INTRODUCTION

Modern life is full of challenges and we all get stressed from time to time. We are pulled in different directions as we balance the demands of work and family, juggle our finances, keep up with the housework and cope with the daily commute. Our bodies are designed to cope with some short-term stress, but when it continues over weeks and months it can cause physical, mental and emotional problems. These problems make us feel tired, depressed and unwell – and even more stressed.

Of course we need to address the sources of our stress, but this may involve life changes that we can't achieve overnight. There is, however, one change that works instantly – taking control of what we eat and drink. By choosing the right foods, we can get our bodies back to a place of calm, so that both physically and emotionally we are much better equipped to deal with whatever life has in store. There are loads of delicious, nutritious foods that positively support all the body systems during periods of stress and target the symptoms that accompany stress. We can literally eat ourselves calm.

The science of stress

The body's initial reaction to stress is known as the 'fight or flight' response, because it provides the rush of energy we might need to confront or run away from a dangerous situation. Our brains trigger the release of the hormones adrenaline, noradrenaline and cortisol, which speed up the heart and breathing rates. Blood is diverted away from the digestive system, skin and organs such as the kidneys, and sent to the muscles where it might be needed to take physical action. The mouth will feel dry, we may sweat more, our hearts are racing – but we can deal with the stress.

If the stressful situation continues, different hormones swing into action to increase our blood sugar levels, giving us prolonged energy, and raising our blood pressure to help us maintain circulation. We can manage like this for a while but if we remain stressed over a long period, the body becomes exhausted because so many of its systems are being forced to overwork, while vital organs are being deprived of the nutrients they need for healthy function.

In short, our bodies are designed to cope with short bursts of stress caused by physical threat; they are ill-equipped to deal with the long-term mental and emotional stresses that we often experience in the modern world.

The long-term effects of stress

- Prolonged high levels of the stress hormone cortisol depress the immune system, so we are more likely to catch any bugs going round.
- Blood sugar levels fluctuate, affecting energy levels and mood.
- If blood pressure is high for too long it causes changes in the arteries, which means blood pressure doesn't drop again even when the stress has passed.
- Stress leads to raised levels of cholesterol in the blood, which is linked to heart and circulatory disease.
- The digestive system becomes sluggish, inflamed and prone to cramps and bloating. It has trouble absorbing the nutrients in our food.
- Cortisol makes us lay down fat round our waists, which is linked to heart disorders.
- We sleep badly, which means the body doesn't have time to recharge.
- All of this plays havoc with hormones and brain function, causing a host of emotional symptoms such as anxiety, depression and mood swings.

How to eat yourself calm

1. Keep blood sugar levels steady

When you are very stressed, you may find you get cravings for fatty, sugary foods. These give a quick hit of energy, but soon after eating them your blood sugar will dip and you'll feel even more sluggish than before. One of the keys to dealing with stress is to keep your blood sugar as steady as possible and that means eating regular small snacks and meals throughout the day, comprising foods that the body will burn at a slow, steady rate.

The Glycaemic Index rates foods according to their effect on blood sugar. High-GI foods, such as sugary drinks, white bread and sweets, are broken down quickly by the digestive system and cause blood sugar to soar, then plummet. Low-GI foods such as vegetables and pulses give a slow, steady release of energy. These are the foods to choose.

2. Top up the B vitamins

We all know that a range of vitamins and minerals, containing different antioxidants and phytonutrients, are essential for good health. But during stressful periods, B group vitamins are particularly useful because they support the nervous system and brain function and stimulate the production of feel-good hormones such as serotonin. B vitamins can become depleted when we are stressed, making us anxious and depressed, so it's vital to top them up – and eating wholegrains, mushrooms, oily fish, poultry, nuts, vegetables and pulses is the best way.

3. Eat lots of antioxidants

Antioxidant vitamins A, C and E are also crucial to boost the immune system and protect the body from the damaging effects of long-term stress. They help to lower blood pressure, protect the heart and digestive system, and encourage brain function. Opt for fruits and vegetables with the brightest colours as these are the ones with the highest antioxidant levels.

4. Look after your digestive system

There are several ways to support your digestive system: eat plenty of fibre-rich foods to prevent constipation, drink loads of water to flush it all through, and include plenty of probiotic live yogurt in your diet to boost levels of healthy bacteria in your gut. Junk foods, such as burgers, pizzas and fry-ups, give the digestive system a heavy load, so avoid them while your system is under strain.

5. Promote restful sleep

Getting a good night's sleep makes everything look better the next day, and it is also essential for regulating hormones, maintaining healthy blood pressure, balancing mood, improving energy levels and keeping a strong immune system. Calcium, magnesium and certain amino acids aid restful sleep and you'll find them in abundance in the recipes in this book.

6. Reduce caffeine and alcohol

Caffeine is a stimulant and produces many of the same effects on the body as stress hormones, so when you are trying to reduce stress, it makes sense to stick to one or two cups of coffee a day, and avoid caffeine in the evenings. Alcohol is a depressant and, while you won't have refreshing sleep after drinking a lot, one glass of red wine from time to time can have health benefits from the antioxidants it contains.

Achieving inner calm

The moment you start eating stress-reducing foods, you will feel the benefits. Your energy, mood and concentration will improve, and gradually the niggling symptoms of stress will disappear. Meanwhile, your internal organs will be functioning more healthily so you will be less prone to infections and long-term life-threatening disease. Follow the meal planner on pages 30–33, or use the problem solver on pages 26–29 to identify the key ingredients that will address your specific symptoms. Find them in the section on superfoods, pages 12–25, to discover how you can include them in your meals.

Of course, diet alone won't solve everything that may be problematic in your life. If you have a tyrannical boss, a hectic work- and home-life schedule, credit-card meltdown or a leaking roof, improving your diet won't take these issues away – but it will make you feel calmer and give you the energy you need to take them on. Your energy and focus will improve, and the niggling symptoms that have blighted your life will disappear. You'll be able to deal with problems more effectively, thereby reducing stress even further. So to achieve that win–win situation, this book is the perfect guide.

CALM
SUPERFOODS

SUPERFOODS

These functional foods support your health on all levels and offer long-term protection against high blood pressure and other stress-related conditions.

Dark chocolate

- ✔ Lowers blood pressure and cholesterol
- ✔ Balances blood sugar
- ✔ Reduces stress hormones
- ✔ Lifts mood
- ✔ Boosts energy

Eating just 40 g (1½ oz) of dark chocolate every day lowers levels of the stress hormone cortisol, as well as the 'fight or flight' hormones released by our adrenal glands when we are under pressure. Choose bars with at least 70 per cent cocoa solids.

It's rich in...

- → Antioxidants, to boost immunity and encourage heart health
- → Phenethylamine, a natural ingredient that is released in the brain when we experience positive emotions
- → Oleic acid, a cholesterol-busting fat
- → Magnesium, to ease headaches, fatigue and palpitations
- → Iron, to even mood, ease headaches and boost energy

Use in... sauces and stews; grate on to fresh fruit or yogurt; snack on a handful of chocolate-covered brazil nuts, or just nibble a couple of small squares as an after-dinner treat. But remember: chocolate does contain sugar and fat, and can play havoc with weight and blood sugar levels.

SEE: CHOCOLATE & ALMOND SQUARES, P63; DARK CHOCOLATE FONDUE WITH FRUIT & NUTS, P122; SOUR CHERRY CHOCOLATE BROWNIE PUDDING, P124.

Mango

✔ Regulates blood pressure
✔ Reduces stress hormones
✔ Boosts immunity
✔ Improves memory
✔ Eases digestion

The bright orange flesh of a single ripe mango contains more than three times the vitamin C of a glass of orange juice, and has been shown to regulate stress hormones and blood pressure. Rich in iron, mango will also improve energy levels.

It's rich in...

➔ Antioxidants and phenols, which protect against heart disease and stroke
➔ Prebiotics and fibre, to encourage healthy digestion
➔ Potassium, to ease palpitations and lower blood pressure
➔ Vitamin C, for immunity, heart, eyes and skin
➔ Vitamin B6 for relaxation, stress reduction and increased energy

Use in... salads with feta cheese, chicken and pecans; top with mascarpone cheese, honey and cinnamon and grill until bubbling; blend with raspberries and/ or yogurt for an instant, stress-busting breakfast; toss into curries and tagines; or eat fresh and ripe, on the stone.

SEE: APRICOT, MANGO & PINEAPPLE SMOOTHIE, P62; FRUITY MANGO FLAPJACKS, P64; GINGERED TOFU & MANGO SALAD, P80; FISH & MANGO CURRY WITH BROWN RICE, P88; MANGO BRÛLÉE, P108.

Oats

✔ Support the nervous system
✔ Lift energy levels and relieve fatigue
✔ Encourage healthy digestion
✔ Promote restful sleep

Oats have long been recognized for their positive impact on the nervous system and, when eaten regularly, have been shown to reduce the effects of stress and relieve fatigue. Oats soothe the digestive system and contain lots of protein to encourage overall health and to help stabilize blood sugar and energy levels.

They are rich in...

➔ Soluble fibre, to lower blood cholesterol and aid digestion
➔ B vitamins, to stimulate the production of the feel-good hormone serotonin
➔ Calcium, potassium and vitamin A, essential for a healthy nervous system
➔ Magnesium, to counter irritability and anxiety, and soothe headaches
➔ Slow-release carbohydrates, which provide long-term energy
➔ Phytonutrients (plant chemicals), to protect the body from chronic diseases like cancer and heart disease

Use in... porridge, or sprinkle on cereal, yogurt and fruit; add oats to your fruit crumble toppings and snack on oat bars or flapjacks to keep energy levels high. Throw a handful into soups, stews and casseroles, and make a savoury crumble topping for fish pie.

SEE: APPLE & YOGURT MUESLI, P36; BLUEBERRY & OAT MUFFINS, P40; BREAKFAST CEREAL BARS, P43.

Salmon

✔ Supports the nervous system
✔ Eases inflammation
✔ Aids memory and concentration
✔ Lifts mood

Salmon is rich in all-important B vitamins which fight stress, encourage a healthy nervous system and help produce the happy brain chemical serotonin. The omega oils it contains have been shown to reduce levels of adrenaline and other stress hormones.

It's rich in...

→ Omega oils, which ease inflammation, improve brain function, and reduce the risk of heart disease and stroke
→ DHA (docosahexaenoic acid), known to reduce depression and improve mood and cognition
→ Selenium, for healthy heart and joints
→ Vitamins B6 and B12, to reduce the emotional and physical effects of stress
→ Vitamin D and certain proteins that reduce inflammation causing headaches and other aches and pains

Use in... scrambled eggs for a high-protein, stress-busting breakfast; toss flakes into pasta dishes, risottos and herby salads; or serve on rye bread with light mayonnaise and a little chopped dill. Poach and top with a scraping of pesto; roast in the oven with fresh asparagus; or make into fishcakes or burgers.

SEE: HERBY SMOKED SALMON OMELETTE, P48; SALMON & ASPARAGUS ROLL-UPS, P50; PUY LENTILS WITH FLAKED SALMON, P72; SALMON WITH BEAN & CELERIAC MASH, P90.

Ginger

✔ Eases digestive complaints
✔ Reduces muscle pain and inflammation
✔ Improves mood
✔ Encourages the absorption of nutrients

Numerous studies have shown the impact of ginger on symptoms of stress. It boosts libido and mood, acts as an analgesic for headaches and muscle pain, and settles a stressed digestive system. It's also rich in nutrients that encourage immunity and ease the impact of stress hormones on the nervous system.

It's rich in...

→ Gingerol, a phytonutrient which has been shown to reduce muscle pain by 25 per cent, ease tension-related headaches, improve digestion by stimulating taste buds and saliva, and reduce nausea
→ Antioxidants, to boost the immune system
→ Vitamin B6, to protect against the emotional and physical effects of stress
→ Chemicals that protect the brain from unhealthy blood sugar levels, which can be caused by prolonged stress

Use in... hot lemon and ginger tea; grate into curries and soups for extra warming zest; add to stir-fries and stir into fruit salads; mix with honey and use to flavour natural live yogurt.

SEE: GINGERED TOFU & MANGO SALAD, P80; THAI MUSSEL CURRY WITH GINGER, P92; ROOT VEGETABLE TAGINE WITH POMEGRANATE SALSA, P94; GINGERY CHICKPEA CURRY, P96.

Turkey

✔ Encourages restful sleep
✔ Reduces anxiety
✔ Lifts mood
✔ Regulates nervous system function

The amino acids contained in turkey not only promote a feeling of calm and even sleepiness, but they are also responsible for improving mood and regulating your sleep cycle. Low in saturated fats, it's a healthy alternative to many types of meat, and the B vitamins it contains help the body to process fats, thus easing digestion.

It's rich in...

➔ Tryptophan, to encourage the release of the feel-good chemical serotonin which lifts mood and aids sleep
➔ Phenylalanine, an amino acid which helps to prevent depression
➔ Vitamins B3 and B6, to support the nervous system. They become depleted in times of stress
➔ Selenium, to promote the healthy function of the immune system
➔ Protein, to balance blood sugar and provide amino acids to aid tissue repair

Use in... crunchy salads, with nuts, dried fruit and cubes of sweet potato; grill, mix with a little fresh salsa, sprinkle with cheese and fill wholewheat tortillas; mix minced turkey with tarragon and chives to create delicious burgers; dice and add to a breakfast frittata instead of bacon.

SEE: TURKEY, PEANUT & MANGO SALAD, P83; WILD RICE & TURKEY SALAD, P84; TURKEY CROQUE MADAME, P86; TURKEY BURGERS WITH SWEET POTATO WEDGES, P102.

Brazil nuts

✔ Stabilize mood
✔ Balance hormones
✔ Improve energy levels and memory
✔ Prevent anxiety

Brazil nuts are the best natural source of selenium, a mineral with a host of health benefits, many of which relate to stress and its symptoms. These nuts are also rich in healthy fats that can reduce inflammation and the risk of heart disease, as well as B vitamins that directly affect the health of the nervous system.

They are rich in...

➔ Zinc, which is drained by chronic stress and anxiety, and boosts healthy immunity, libido, hormone balance, energy levels and memory
➔ Selenium, which helps to balance mood and prevent anxiety and depression
➔ B vitamins, to reduce the impact of stress on the mind and body
➔ Omega oils, to ease inflammation and promote heart health
➔ Magnesium, to ensure better absorption of energy from food and ensure healthy nerve function

Use in... your morning muesli – just a handful gives you the full recommended daily allowance of selenium; dip in dark chocolate for extra stress relief; toss into a salad with romaine lettuce, cubes of feta cheese and a handful of sultanas; coarsely chop and add to toppings for crumbles or casseroles.

SEE: CRANBERRY & APPLE CRUMBLE, P114; DARK CHOCOLATE FONDUE WITH FRUIT & NUTS, P122.

Blueberries

- ✔ Improve energy levels
- ✔ Reduce blood pressure
- ✔ Decrease the physical and emotional impact of stress
- ✔ Reduce inflammation
- ✔ Enhance concentration and memory

Something of a superstar in the superfood arena, blueberries have a wealth of benefits and very high levels of antioxidants which repair and protect your body from the effects of stress. Blueberries also boost energy levels and balance moods, making it that much easier to deal with the stress in your life.

They are rich in...

- → Antioxidant nutrients, such as anthocyanins, which lower blood pressure, protect the nervous system and digestive tract, encourage optimum brain function and balance blood sugar
- → Vitamin C, to boost immunity and reduce the impact of the stress hormone cortisol, affecting both body and mind
- → Fibre, to balance blood sugar levels
- → B vitamins, to boost metabolism and energy levels, and encourage a healthy nervous system

Use in... your morning cereal; blitz in a food processor with natural yogurt and a little honey for a delicious fruit fool; add to pancakes or wholegrain muffins; use frozen blueberries as the basis for smoothies; toss in a salad with a little goats' cheese and sliced almonds.

SEE: BLUEBERRY & OAT MUFFINS, P40; BLUEBERRY & LEMON ICE CREAM, P110; BLUEBERRY FOOL, P120.

Pistachios

- ✔ Reduce the effects of high blood pressure
- ✔ Balance blood sugar
- ✔ Encourage heart health
- ✔ Ease inflammation
- ✔ Boost energy levels

Pistachios are packed with essential nutrients, with high levels of magnesium and B vitamins that give your immune system a boost and healthy fats that help protect your heart.

They are rich in...

- → Vitamins A and E, which can help to prevent inflammation which causes digestive disturbances, aches and pains
- → Omega oils, to reduce inflammation, encourage brain and heart health, and support the immune system
- → Vitamin B6, which is essential for the supply of oxygenated blood to maintain energy levels and is also required for healthy immunity and nervous system
- → Protein, fibre and healthy fats, to balance blood sugar

Use in... fruit and vegetable salads for colour and crunch; gently roast to enhance the omega-3 content and eat as the perfect snack; add to muesli or sprinkle over cereal or yogurt; stir-fry with chicken, crunchy vegetables and ginger; crush to make a crust for lamb or beef before roasting.

SEE: APRICOT PURÉE WITH YOGURT & PISTACHIOS, P39; BAKED BANANAS, P112; BLUEBERRY FOOL, P120.

Apricots

✔ Ease muscle tension and headaches
✔ Reduce palpitations
✔ Boost the immune system
✔ Protect against damage caused
   by stress
✔ Boost energy

Apricots contain high levels of magnesium, the 'anti-stress' mineral that decreases the release of the stress hormone cortisol. They are rich in antioxidants which help to protect the body from the impact of stress, and contain plenty of iron to help your red blood cells carry fatigue-busting oxygen throughout your body.

They are rich in...

→ Magnesium, to reduce heart palpitations, relax muscles, encourage restful sleep and support a healthy nervous system
→ Fibre, to encourage healthy digestion and absorption of nutrients from food
→ Beta-carotene and lycopene, antioxidants, which encourage heart health and boost immunity
→ Iron, for boosting immunity and energy levels

Use in... both savoury and sweet salads; dried apricots are delicious in chicken dishes for a Middle Eastern flavour; stir into wholegrain pancake batter; blend with a frozen banana and live natural yogurt for an energy-boosting smoothie; stew with water and a little honey for a delicious breakfast compote.

SEE: APRICOT PURÉE WITH YOGURT & PISTACHIOS, P39; APRICOT, MANGO & PINEAPPLE SMOOTHIE, P62.

Spinach

✔ Prevents blood pressure surges
✔ Relaxes muscles
✔ Encourages restorative sleep
✔ Reduces anxiety
✔ Regulates stress hormones
✔ Promotes wellbeing

Spinach not only aids relaxation and promotes a feeling of calm, largely due to its high magnesium content, but it is rich in iron to fight fatigue, and helps to mop up excess cortisol levels in the bloodstream. Folic acid and other B vitamins encourage a healthy nervous system, and even aid concentration and memory.

It's rich in...

→ Fibre, to balance blood sugar and encourage healthy digestion
→ Anti-inflammatory chemicals neoxanthin and violaxanthin, which reduce inflammation and pain
→ Peptides, to lower blood pressure
→ Vitamin K, for a healthy nervous system and brain function

Use in... soups, stews and casseroles, adding it towards the end of cooking; use instead of lettuce in sandwiches and salads; add to cheese and chives for a light omelette filling; blend with ricotta cheese, garlic and lightly steamed butternut squash for a delicious pasta sauce or topping for backed potatoes.

SEE: WARM SPINACH SALAD, P79; ROOT VEGETABLE TAGINE WITH POMEGRANATE SALSA, P94.

Sweet potatoes

✔ Reduce inflammation
✔ Regulate blood sugar levels
✔ Encourage healthy digestion
✔ Encourage relaxation
✔ Lift mood

A great source of fibre, sweet potatoes can ease digestive complaints and steady blood sugar levels. Their bright colour indicates a wealth of antioxidant vitamins and other key chemicals which can help to reduce the impact of stress on your body and mind, and prevent inflammatory conditions often associated with stress.

They are rich in...
→ Vitamin B6, to support the nervous system, encourage relaxation and prevent heart disease
→ Vitamin C, to help reduce the stress hormone cortisol in the body, boost immunity and ease digestion
→ Vitamin D, to encourage the health of your heart and nerves, ease fatigue and balance moods
→ Magnesium, to promote restful sleep and aid relaxation

Use in... soups, curries, casseroles and stews; mash with a little half-fat crème fraîche and pepper as a delicious side dish; roast sweet potato wedges in olive oil as an alternative to chips; cook in their jackets and top with tuna mixed with a little Greek yogurt, the juice of a lime and a handful of chopped coriander.

SEE: SWEET POTATO & CABBAGE SOUP, P66; ROOT VEGETABLE TAGINE WITH POMEGRANATE SALSA, P94; WILD MUSHROOM STROGANOFF & SWEET POTATO MASH, P98; BAKED SWEET POTATOES WITH VEGETABLE CHILLI, P100.

Apples

✔ Balance blood sugar
✔ Support the liver
✔ Reduce the stress hormone cortisol
✔ Ease depression
✔ Encourage digestion

The humble apple contains a host of nutrients that work to reduce the production of the damaging stress hormone cortisol, while having an important balancing effect on blood sugar. Rich in antioxidants, apples will support almost every part of your body in times of stress.

They are rich in...
→ Quercetin, a nutrient which supports the immune system, reduces cortisol production and encourages healthy brain function
→ Phosphorus and iron, which repair damage caused by stress
→ Pectin, a soluble fibre which aids digestion and promotes the health of the digestive tract, as well as balancing blood sugar
→ Sulphur, which helps support liver function

Use in... red cabbage dishes for extra flavour; stuff a chicken breast with apples, walnuts, thyme and wholegrain breadcrumbs; mix with honey and raisins, top with an oat and nut crumble and bake for a satisfying dessert; purée as an accompaniment to pork or grilled mackerel.

SEE: APPLE & YOGURT MUESLI, P36; APPLE, PEAR & CHERRY COMPOTE, P38; GOATS' CHEESE, APPLE & WALNUT SALAD, P76; CRANBERRY & APPLE CRUMBLE, P114.

Grapes

✔ Reduce the risk of high blood pressure
✔ Ease depression
✔ Encourage heart health
✔ Help prevent stomach ulcers
  and indigestion
✔ Improve memory and concentration

Both green and black grapes – particularly the seeds and skins – contain crucial vitamins, minerals and other nutrients which can ease the impact of stress on the body, while encouraging healthy digestion and even easing headaches. Grapes are a traditional remedy for fatigue, probably because of their high iron content.

They are rich in...
→ Manganese and potassium, which lower blood pressure, boost immunity and help prevent depression
→ Resveratrol, which encourages heart health, lowers sugar and fat levels in the blood and reduces blood pressure
→ Beneficial bacteria, which encourage digestion and reduce the risk of stomach ulcers
→ Antioxidant nutrients and chemicals that reduce inflammation, protect the heart and reduce stress-related damage to cells

Use in... salads with a little feta cheese and toasted almonds; freeze grapes for a sweet, refreshing snack; serve halved with walnuts, cooked chicken and lettuce in a honey-yogurt dressing; roast grapes alongside pork; add red grapes, spring onions and sliced apricots to boiled rice and stir in a creamy yogurt dressing.

SEE: GOATS' CHEESE, APPLE & WALNUT SALAD, P76; DARK CHOCOLATE FONDUE WITH FRUIT & NUTS, P122.

Cherries

✔ Reduce inflammation and pain
✔ Aid relaxation and encourage sleep
✔ Boost concentration
✔ Ease depression
✔ Reduce cravings
✔ Enhance libido

Both sweet and sour cherries are packed with nutrients which can affect everything from your sense of wellbeing to your heart health and risk of diabetes. Cherries can ease headaches and tension-related aches and pains, and protect the body against disease and the effects of stress.

They are rich in...
→ Melatonin, a hormone which helps promote restful sleep and has a calming effect
→ Anthocyanins, plant chemicals which block inflammation and pain (including headaches) that cause or are caused by stress
→ Tyrosine, an amino acid which is required for restful sleep, improved mood, virility and concentration
→ Fibre, to control blood sugar and aid digestion

Use in... a morning smoothie with live yogurt; cherry juice – sour cherry juice in particular – will ease digestive problems and headaches quickly; dip in dark chocolate for a delicious, nutritious treat; dried or frozen cherries make a healthy snack; add to wholegrain muffins or pancakes; make a cherry sauce for pork or game dishes.

SEE: CHERRY & CINNAMON PARFAIT, P116; SOUR CHERRY CHOCOLATE BROWNIE PUDDING, P124.

Brown rice

✔ Reduces cortisol levels
✔ Eases anxiety
✔ Balances blood sugar
✔ Eases headaches
✔ Lowers blood pressure
✔ Boosts energy levels

An excellent source of fibre and numerous vitamins and minerals, brown rice also contains plenty of tryptophan, the amino acid that increases serotonin and melatonin levels in the body, encouraging a sense of wellbeing and restful sleep. It acts like a brush in the digestive tract, and encourages the absorption of nutrients.

It's rich in...

→ B vitamins, to support the nervous system, encourage even moods and improve concentration
→ Manganese, for a healthy nervous system and energy production
→ Selenium, to encourage immunity, balance moods and promote heart health
→ Magnesium, to relax the nervous system, reduce blood pressure, lower the incidence of headaches, prevent muscle spasms and encourage restful sleep

Use in... a delicious salad with berries, seeds, nuts, spring onions, herbs and a light vinaigrette dressing; make brown rice pudding with soya milk, cinnamon, nutmeg, sultanas and honey; stir in sautéed mushrooms and leeks for a delicious side dish; top with grilled chicken, fresh salsa and grated cheese for a Mexican-style treat.

SEE: MEDITERRANEAN BROWN RICE SALAD, P82; BROWN RICE PUDDING, P113.

Mushrooms

✔ Balance blood sugar levels
✔ Improve health of the liver and endocrine (hormonal) system
✔ Lift mood
✔ Encourage immunity

A rich source of protective, mood-lifting selenium, mushrooms retain their nutrients no matter how they are cooked. They contain natural insulin, which helps to balance blood sugar levels and restore a sense of calm.

They are rich in...

→ Polysaccharides, which have been shown to boost the immune system
→ Copper, to produce blood cells and maintain heart health
→ Potassium, to lower blood pressure and reduce the risk of stroke
→ Niacin, to encourage the health of the nervous system

Use in... stews, soups, stir-fries and casseroles; sauté in a little olive oil and parsley, and add to omelettes or frittatas; slice and toss into a warm spinach salad; pan-fry with garlic and shallots and serve on wholegrain toast.

SEE: SCRAMBLED EGGS ON GRILLED MUSHROOMS, P46; BACON & MUSHROOM FRITTATA, P47; GRILLED MUSHROOM & GARLIC WRAPS, P69; CHICKEN & BARLEY RISOTTO, P105; WARM SPINACH SALAD, P79; WILD MUSHROOM STROGANOFF & SWEET POTATO MASH, P98.

Beetroot

✔ Aphrodisiac
✔ Aids relaxation
✔ Encourages a sense of wellbeing
✔ Lowers blood pressure
✔ Boosts energy levels
✔ Promotes nervous system health

Beetroot is an abundant source of dozens of vitamins and minerals, and is one of the richest sources of energy-boosting iron. It contains betaine and tryptophan to ease depression and lift mood.

It's rich in...

→ Folate, which helps to build tissue and red blood cells, boosting energy levels
→ Betalains, plant chemicals which have strong anti-inflammatory and antioxidant properties
→ Nitrates, which have been shown to lower stress-related high blood pressure within an hour
→ Boron, which can help to improve virility in both men and women

Use in... borscht, an Eastern European soup; roast and top with feta cheese and toasted walnuts for a delicious, nutritious salad; juice and serve on crushed ice for a mood-boosting breakfast or snack; roast until tender, purée with a dash of horseradish and serve with toasted pitta bread or crudités.

SEE: ROASTED BEETROOT & FETA SALAD WITH ALMONDS, P74; MEDITERRANEAN BROWN RICE SALAD, P82; ROOT VEGETABLE TAGINE WITH POMEGRANATE SALSA, P94.

Avocado

✔ Reduces cholesterol
✔ Regulates blood pressure
✔ Boosts immunity
✔ Eases digestion
✔ Balances blood sugar levels
✔ Increases absorption of nutrients from other foods

Avocado contains more than 25 key nutrients, including B vitamins and potassium, to encourage the health of your nervous system. The healthy fats it contains can help to promote heart health, while regulating blood pressure. It contains high levels of vitamin E to boost immunity and improve skin health.

It's rich in...
➔ Beta-sitosterol, to lower unhealthy cholesterol
➔ Potassium, to control blood pressure
➔ Fibre and monounsaturated fats, to balance blood sugar levels and prevent insulin resistance, a common side-effect of stress
➔ Folic acid, pantothenic acid and vitamin K, to reduce stress levels and improve the health of the nervous system

Use in... spinach salads, to increase the uptake of nutrients by up to 200 per cent; chop with a little fresh chilli, diced onion and tomato for an instant guacamole; purée into smoothies for an energy-boosting snack; stuff with chopped egg and top with chives for an easy, satisfying lunch.

SEE: GUACAMOLE WITH TORTILLA BITES, P54; AVOCADO WITH YOGURT DRESSING, P57; WARM SPINACH SALAD, P79.

Eggs

✔ Promote heart health
✔ Regulate mood
✔ Encourage alertness
✔ Boost health of nerves and brain
✔ Raise energy levels
✔ Support adrenal glands

Very few foods are as rich in key nutrients as eggs, and their high protein levels not only balance blood sugar, but also provide a good source of sustainable energy. Rich in B vitamins to support the nervous system, eggs are undoubtedly an essential part of any anti-stress diet.

They are rich in...
➔ Tryptophan, which helps to regulate mood and encourages sleep
➔ Tyrosine, which promotes mental activity and concentration
➔ Protein, to encourage overall health and to help stabilize blood sugar and energy levels
➔ Pantothenic acid, the 'anti-stress vitamin', which supports the adrenal glands

Use in... lightly cooked omelettes stuffed with spinach and mushrooms; boiled eggs; poach and serve on smoked salmon and wholegrain toast; braise in chopped tomatoes and chilli for a nutritious Mexican breakfast; scramble and wrap in a soft flour tortilla for an easy lunch or breakfast burrito; boil and mash with a little live yogurt and dill and serve on a bed of lettuce or a slice of wholegrain bread.

SEE: TURKISH POACHED EGGS WITH YOGURT, P44; SCRAMBLED EGGS ON GRILLED MUSHROOMS, P46; BACON & MUSHROOM FRITTATA, P47; HERBY SMOKED SALMON OMELETTE, P48; STUFFED EGGS, P60.

Cinnamon

✔ Controls blood sugar levels
✔ Boosts immunity
✔ Encourages brain function
✔ Protects against heart disease
✔ Reduces inflammation
✔ Reduces levels of the stress hormone cortisol

Cinnamon has long been used for medicinal purposes, and studies have found that it not only lowers blood sugar levels, but also boosts energy levels and eases the impact of stress. Its smell has been shown to improve brain function and memory.

It's rich in...

→ MCHP, a chemical that reduces blood sugar levels and some forms of anxiety
→ Anti-inflammatory chemicals, which promote heart health, protect arteries from stress-related damage and reduce muscle and joint pain
→ Calcium, to ease anxiety and restore nervous system function
→ Essential oils that boost immunity and encourage healthy digestion

Use in... porridge; stir into warm, freshly pressed apple juice; use to flavour unsweetened fruit purées and serve with live yogurt; add a teaspoon to chicken and lamb casseroles for warmth and flavour; steep cinnamon sticks in boiling water to make a nutritious, stimulating tea; sprinkle over mashed bananas and serve on wholemeal toast.

SEE: EDAMAME BEAN HUMMUS, P58; ROOT VEGETABLE TAGINE WITH POMEGRANATE SALSA, P94; MANGO BRÛLÉE, P108; BROWN RICE PUDDING, P113; CRANBERRY & APPLE CRUMBLE, P114; CHERRY & CINNAMON PARFAIT, P116.

Cranberries

✔ Balance blood sugar levels
✔ Encourage heart health
✔ Reduce inflammation
✔ Protect the brain from stress-related damage
✔ Boost immunity
✔ Encourage healthy digestion

Cranberries are one of the richest sources of vitamin C and other antioxidant nutrients, which play an important role in reducing the damaging effects of stress, while encouraging overall health and wellbeing. Full of fibre, they help regulate digestion and blood sugar levels.

They are rich in...

→ Phytonutrients, which reduce inflammation, ease muscle and joint pain and improve oral health, digestion and heart health
→ Proanthocyanidins, proven to boost immunity
→ Resveratrol, piceatannol and pterostilbene, which can help to prevent heart and circulatory damage caused by stress
→ Chemicals that can help to prevent stomach ulcers

Use in... chicken or lamb stews or tagines; add dried cranberries to your breakfast cereal or muesli; mix with apples and cinnamon and top with oats for a tasty crumble, juice, sweeten with a little maple syrup and gently heat for a nourishing warm drink; toss dried cranberries into a salad with dark green leaves and goats' cheese; fill the core of an apple with cranberries and a little brown sugar and cinnamon and bake for a tangy, healthy dessert.

SEE: CRANBERRY & APPLE CRUMBLE, P114.

Live yogurt

✔ Encourages healthy digestion
✔ Reduces risk of high blood pressure
✔ Increases the absorption of stress-relieving B vitamins
✔ Boosts immunity
✔ Enables restful sleep
✔ Eases anxiety

Yogurt rich in probiotics (healthy bacteria) is often tolerated by people who are intolerant to lactose. It is a great source of calcium and B vitamins. By encouraging the health of the gut, yogurt can improve digestion, immunity and even emotional health, by promoting communication between the gut and the brain.

It's rich in...

➔ Friendly bacteria, which encourage the health of the gut, help it absorb nutrients more efficiently and enhance immune function
➔ Probiotics, which have been shown to impact the brain chemistry involved in stress, anxiety and depression
➔ Calcium, which acts on the nervous system and encourages restful sleep
➔ B vitamins, for a healthy nervous system and improved relaxation

Use in... fruit smoothies; mix with chives, sea salt and black pepper to top baked potatoes; use instead of milk on cereal and muesli; blend with herbs, spices and a little olive oil for a creamy dip; add lemon juice, lemon rind and dill to make a satisfying salad dressing; stir into soups and curries instead of cream or coconut milk.

SEE: APPLE AND YOGURT MUESLI, P36;
APPLE, PEAR & CHERRY COMPOTE, P38;
TURKISH POACHED EGGS WITH YOGURT, P44;
RASPBERRY YOGURT GRATIN, P121.

Popcorn

✔ Encourages healthy digestion
✔ Balances blood sugar
✔ Protects against stress-related diseases
✔ Boosts energy levels

Amazingly, popcorn contains more antioxidants than fruit and vegetables and, as a wholegrain, it is an excellent source of B vitamins, fibre, slow-release carbohydrates and good-quality protein. Watch the salt and the butter, which can add unnecessary calories.

It's rich in...

➔ Polyphenols, antioxidant plant chemicals, which can protect the body from disease and stress-related damage
➔ Ferulic acid, which protects against cancer, diabetes, cardiovascular problems and diseases of the nervous system
➔ Fibre, for healthy digestion and enhanced absorption of nutrients from food
➔ B vitamins, to improve nerve function and help the body produce energy efficiently

Use in... salads and soups instead of croûtons; mist with olive oil and season with a little sea salt and lots of black pepper as a snack; flavour with finely chopped fresh herbs, like dill, coriander and parsley; for a sweet treat, drizzle with a little maple syrup and throw in a handful of chopped almonds; sprinkle with ground cinnamon or ginger, for added zing; crush and use as a coating for chicken or fish, in place of breadcrumbs or flour.

Almonds

✔ Stabilize blood sugar levels
✔ Lower bad cholesterol
✔ Boost energy levels
✔ Promote relaxation
✔ Protect your heart

Almonds contain more nutrients than any other nut, and are an excellent source of vitamin E, calcium, magnesium, phosphorus and iron, all of which play a role in coping with the stresses of day-to-day life, and encourage a sense of calm. The healthy fats they contain help to prevent heart disease and decrease inflammation in the body.

They are rich in...
→ Vitamin E, an antioxidant which has been shown to prevent damage caused by stress, while boosting immunity
→ B vitamins and magnesium, which help produce serotonin, regulating mood and relieving the symptoms of stress
→ Zinc, which fights the negative effects of stress
→ Calcium, to promote restful sleep and encourage relaxation

Use in... salads with cheese and dried fruit; spread almond butter on toast; use almond milk on cereal or in hot drinks; add to muesli or crumble toppings; coat chicken breasts or fish with ground almonds; make almond pesto, using almonds in place of pine nuts.

SEE: ROASTED BEETROOT & FETA SALAD WITH ALMONDS, P74; BAKED BANANAS, P112; CRANBERRY & APPLE CRUMBLE, P114; RICOTTA, PLUM & ALMOND CAKE, P118; DARK CHOCOLATE FONDUE WITH FRUIT & NUTS, P122.

Bananas

✔ Protect the nervous system
✔ Encourage heart health
✔ Lift mood
✔ Promote a sense of calm
✔ Boost energy

Bananas are effectively little packets of energy, with a host of key nutrients to help your body work at optimum level. Most importantly, they provide plenty of potassium (often deficient in the Western diet), which is required for a healthy nervous system and balanced moods.

They are rich in...
→ Potassium, which improves the health of your heart and nervous system; potassium also helps to lower blood pressure
→ Tryptophan, to help the body produce serotonin, which has a calming effect on the brain
→ Vitamin B6, to encourage the production of oxygen-carrying red blood cells and disease-fighting antibodies
→ Fibre, to improve digestion and balance blood sugar levels

Use in... fruit smoothies; fruit salads; mashed on wholegrain toast with a sprinkling of cinnamon; baked with a dash of vanilla and some maple syrup, served with live yogurt; grill and serve alongside duck or teriyaki pork chops.

SEE: BAKED BANANAS, P112.

WHAT'S YOUR PROBLEM?

Relieve symptoms of stress by eating the foods that target them. Decide which symptoms affect you and choose from the foods and recipes that can relieve them. There is an icon by each symptom. These icons are used throughout the recipe section to highlight which recipes can help combat which symptoms.

Headaches

Wholegrains, salmon, olive oil, ginger, nuts, seeds, berries, cucumber, melon, tomatoes, grapefruit, apricots, papaya, peaches, cinnamon, rosemary, oats

Recipes Include:
Apricot purée with yogurt & pistachios, p39; Salmon with bean & celeriac mash, p90; Gingery chickpea curry, p96; Cranberry & apple crumble, p114.

Muscle tension/ pain

Ginger, salmon, sour cherries, yogurt, eggs, peanuts, turkey, lentils, almonds

Recipes Include:
Apple, pear & cherry compote, p38; Turkish poached eggs with yogurt, p44; Puy lentils with flaked salmon, p72; Root vegetable tagine with pomegranate salsa, p94; Sour cherry chocolate brownie pudding, p124.

Digestive problems (diarrhoea/ tummy ache/ indigestion/ constipation)

Salmon, ginger, bananas, rye bread, cinnamon, apples, spinach, edamame beans (soya), sweet potatoes, yogurt, berries, avocado, barley, flaxseed, brown rice

Recipes Include:
Apple & yogurt muesli, p36; Tzatziki with rye toast, p52; Warm spinach salad, p79; Mediterranean brown rice salad, p82.

Dizziness

Poultry, pulses, eggs, tofu, yogurt, fish, wholegrains, bananas, peaches, apricots, spinach, asparagus, peas

Recipes Include:
Salmon & asparagus roll-ups, p50; Turkey burgers with sweet potato wedges, p102; Chicken & barley risotto, p105; Baked bananas, p112.

Breathlessness

Nuts, seeds, pulses, dried apricots, raisins, sultanas, spinach, lean red meat, broccoli
Recipes Include: Apricot, mango & pineapple smoothie, p62; Goats' cheese, apple & walnut salad, p76; Lamb & flageolet bean stew, p106; Dark chocolate fondue with fruit & nuts, p122.

High blood pressure

Skimmed milk, spinach, sunflower seeds, beans, baked potatoes, bananas, edamame beans (soya), salmon, dark chocolate
Recipes Include: Edamame bean hummus, p58; Chocolate & almond squares, p63; Gingered tofu & mango salad, p80; Potato & onion tortilla, p97.

Irritability

Tuna, salmon, mackerel, oats, black beans, pumpkin seeds, artichokes, dark chocolate, spinach, bananas, peanuts, brown rice, cashews
Recipes Include: Fruity mango flapjacks, p64; Smoked mackerel pasta salad, p73; Turkey, peanut & mango salad, p83; Wild mushroom stroganoff & sweet potato mash, p98.

Poor concentration & forgetfulness

Broccoli, Brussels sprouts, cauliflower, spinach, berries, cherries, blackcurrants, aubergine, onions, red apples, beetroot, leeks, apricots, grapes, lentils, edamame beans (soya), oranges, fish, dark chocolate, wholegrains
Recipes Include: Edamame bean hummus, p58; Roasted beetroot & feta salad with almonds, p74.

Anxiety

Brazil nuts, peaches, blueberries, acacia berries, almonds, dark chocolate, oats, brown rice, edamame beans (soya), bananas, peanuts, avocado, melon, lettuce, raspberries, broad beans

Recipes Include: Apple & yogurt muesli, p36; Guacamole with tortilla bites, p54; Chocolate & almond squares, p63; Warm spinach salad, p79; Blueberry fool, p120.

Mood swings

Wholegrains, pulses, tuna, salmon, halibut, cheese, yogurt, green tea, dark chocolate, mushrooms, almonds, brazil nuts, pistachios, blueberries, pomegranate, cinnamon, leafy green vegetables

Recipes Include: Herby smoked salmon omelette, p48; Grilled mushroom & garlic wraps, p69; Wild mushroom stroganoff & sweet potato mash, p98.

Depression/ unhappiness

Salmon, wholegrains, oats, nuts, seeds, pulses, brown rice, brewer's yeast (or Marmite), quinoa, cabbage, brazil nuts, dark chocolate, sweet potatoes, kiwi, peppers, oranges, carrots, melon, apricots

Recipes Include: Garlic & flageolet bean pâté, p56; Bacon & cannellini bean soup, p68; Root vegetable tagine with pomegranate salsa, p94.

Chest pains/ palpitations

Wholegrains, nuts, seeds, salmon, mackerel, fresh fruit and vegetables

Recipes Include: Apricot, mango & pineapple smoothie, p62; Smoked mackerel pasta salad, p73; Baked sweet potatoes with vegetable chilli, p100; Herby quinoa with lemon & chicken, p104.

Frequent colds & infections

Garlic, potatoes, horseradish, strawberries (and other berries), ginger, yogurt, oats, apricots, asparagus, mangoes, cauliflower, mushrooms, sweet potatoes, shellfish, brazil nuts, peaches, broccoli, sunflower seeds, celery

Recipes Include:
Spicy prawn kebabs with wild rice, p91; Gingery chickpea curry, p96; Mango brûlée, p108.

Loss of libido/desire

Celery, shellfish, pineapple, bananas, avocado, almonds, mangoes, peaches, strawberries, eggs, figs, garlic, dark chocolate

Recipes Include:
Stuffed eggs, p60; Apricot, mango & pineapple smoothie, p62; Lemony scallop skewers with rocket, p70; Thai mussel curry with ginger, p92.

Sleep problems

Popcorn, oats, dairy produce, peanuts, grapes, edamame beans (soya), seeds, pulses, eggs, honey, almonds, avocado, bananas, seafood, turkey, papaya, mushrooms, brown rice

Recipes Include:
Blueberry & oat muffins, p40; Edamame bean hummus, p58; Gingered tofu & mango salad, p80; Turkey burgers with sweet potato wedges, p102.

Low energy

Dried cranberries, pistachios, blueberries, oranges, spinach, salmon, mackerel, almonds, olive oil, green tea, oatmeal, pulses, cinnamon, ginger, garlic, turmeric, brown rice, broccoli, sesame seeds, avocado

Recipes Include:
Puy lentil salad with flaked salmon, p72; Root vegetable tagine with pomegranate salsa, p94; Cranberry & apple crumble, p114.

PUTTING IT ALL TOGETHER

Meal Planner	Monday	Tuesday	Wednesday
Breakfast	Breakfast cereal bars, p43	Apple & yogurt muesli, p36	Blueberry & oat muffins, p40
Morning snack	Tzatziki with rye toast, p52	Edamame bean hummus, p58	Salmon & asparagus roll-ups, p50
Lunch	Sweet potato & cabbage soup, p66	Wild rice & turkey salad, p84	Bacon & cannellini bean soup, p68
Afternoon snack	Avocado with yogurt dressing, p57	Stuffed eggs, p60	Fruity mango flapjacks, p64
Dinner	Salmon with bean & celeriac mash, p90	Lamb & flageolet bean stew, p106	Wild mushroom stroganoff & sweet potato mash, p98
Dessert	Ricotta, plum & almond cake, p118	Mango brûlée, p108	Raspberry yogurt gratin, p121

Thursday	Friday	Saturday	Sunday
Apricot purée with yogurt & pistachios, p39	Scrambled eggs on grilled mushrooms, p46	Bacon & mushroom frittata, p47	Herby smoked salmon omelette, p48
Chocolate & almond squares, p63	Broccoli florets & carrot sticks with Tzatziki, p52	Apricot, mango & pineapple smoothie, p62	Guacamole with tortilla bites, p54
Goats' cheese, apple & walnut salad, p76	Lemony scallop skewers with rocket, p70	Gingered tofu & mango salad, p80	Warm spinach salad, p79
Popcorn	Black olive tapenade with oatcakes, p53	Dark chocolate covered brazil nuts	A chunk of cheese and a bunch of grapes
Root vegetable tagine with pomegranate salsa, p94	Thai mussel curry with ginger, p92	Potato & onion tortilla, p97	Herby quinoa with lemon & chicken, p104
Brown rice pudding, p113	Sour cherry chocolate brownie pudding, p124	Baked bananas, p112	Cranberry & apple crumble, p114

Meal Planner	Monday	Tuesday	Wednesday
Breakfast	Apple, pear & cherry compote, p38	Quinoa porridge with pomegranate, p42	Scrambled eggs on grilled mushrooms, p46
Morning snack	Garlic & flageolet bean pâté, p56	Salmon & asparagus roll-ups, p50	Black olive tapenade with oatcakes, p53
Lunch	Watermelon & feta salad, p78	Grilled mushroom & garlic wraps, p69	Turkey, peanut & mango salad, p83
Afternoon snack	Stuffed eggs, p60	Popcorn sprinkled with cinnamon	Dark chocolate covered brazil nuts
Dinner	Fish & mango curry with brown rice, p88	Spicy prawn kebabs with wild rice, p91	Gingery chickpea curry, p96
Dessert	Blueberry & lemon ice cream, 110	Dark chocolate fondue with fruit & nuts, p122	Blueberry fool, p120

WEEK 2

Thursday	Friday	Saturday	Sunday
Blueberry & oat muffins, p40	Apple & yogurt muesli, p36	Herby smoked salmon omelette, p48	Turkish poached eggs with yogurt, p44
Apricot, mango & pineapple smoothie, p62	Avocado with yogurt dressing, p57	Edamame bean hummus with rice cakes, p58	Guacamole with tortilla bites, p54
Puy lentils with flaked salmon, p72	Turkey Croque Madame, p86	Roasted beetroot & feta salad with almonds, p74	Mediterranean brown rice salad, p82
Chocolate & almond squares, p63	Banana	Garlic & flageolet bean pâté, p56	Fruity mango flapjacks, p64
Chicken & barley risotto, p105	Baked sweet potatoes with vegetable chilli, p100	Thai mussel curry with ginger, p92	Turkey burgers with sweet potato wedges, p102
Cherry & cinnamon parfait, p116	Brown rice pudding, p113	Ricotta, plum & almond cake, p118	Sour cherry chocolate brownie pudding, p124

CALM
RECIPES

APPLE & YOGURT MUESLI

A filling breakfast to balance blood sugar and provide slow-release energy through the morning.

Preparation time: 15 minutes, plus soaking
Cooking time: 10 minutes
Serves 4

200 g (7 oz) **porridge oats**
25 g (1 oz) **wheat germ**
25 g (1 oz) **rye flakes**
25 g (1 oz) **millet flakes**
50 g (2 oz) **hazelnuts**, coarsely chopped
50 g (2 oz) **almonds**, coarsely chopped
50 g (2 oz) **sultanas**
50 g (2 oz) soft **dried apricots**,
    coarsely chopped
50 g (2 oz) soft **dried dates**,
    coarsely chopped
2 **dessert apples**, peeled
    and coarsely grated
400 ml (14 fl oz) **apple juice**
2 tsps **ground cinnamon**
250 ml (8 fl oz) **fat-free Greek yogurt**
    with honey
2 tsps **golden linseeds**
clear **honey**, to serve (optional)

Place the porridge oats in a large bowl and stir in the wheat germ, rye flakes, millet flakes, nuts and dried fruits. Arrange the mixture on a baking sheet and place in a preheated oven, 160°C (325°F), Gas Mark 3, for 10 minutes then allow to cool.

Return the muesli to the mixing bowl and stir in the apples. Add the apple juice and cinnamon and stir well to combine. Leave to soak for 5–6 minutes.

Divide the soaked muesli between 4 serving bowls and spoon the yogurt on top. Scatter with the linseeds and drizzle with a little honey, if liked.

APPLE, PEAR & CHERRY COMPOTE

This not only makes a healthy breakfast rich in antioxidants and fibre, but it's great served warm as a dessert.

Preparation time: 20 minutes
Cooking time: 20-25 minutes
Serves 6

4 **dessert apples**, peeled, cored and diced
2 **Bramley apples**, peeled, cored and diced
4 **pears**, peeled, cored and diced
3 tbsps light soft **brown sugar**
2 tbsps **water**
½ tsp **vanilla extract**
150 g (5 oz) **dried sour cherries**
live natural yogurt, to serve

Place the apples, pears and sugar in a nonstick saucepan with the measurement water and bring to the boil. Reduce the heat, cover the pan and simmer gently for 15-20 minutes, or until the apples are soft and beginning to break down.

Stir in the vanilla and cherries, add a little more water if necessary, then cover and cook for a further 5 minutes. Taste and add a little more sugar, if required.

Transfer to a blender or food processor and blend to create a chunky compote. Serve warm or cold with live yogurt. The compote can be stored in an airtight container in the refrigerator for up to a week.

APRICOT PURÉE WITH YOGURT & PISTACHIOS

This fruity purée is bursting with stress-busting magnesium. Serve with live yogurt to aid the digestion.

Preparation time: 5 minutes
Cooking time: 25–30 minutes
Serves 6
················

400 g (13 oz) **dried apricots**
325 ml (11 fl oz) **orange juice**
finely grated rind of ½ **orange**

To serve
100 ml (3½ fl oz) **live natural yogurt**
    per person
25 g (1 oz) **raw pistachio nuts**,
    chopped, per person

Place the apricots, orange juice and orange rind in a nonstick saucepan over a medium heat and bring to the boil. Reduce the heat and simmer for 20–25 minutes, or until apricots are plump and juicy.

Remove from the heat, allow to cool slightly, then transfer to a blender or food processor and blend until smooth. Serve warm or cold, layered with yogurt and chopped pistachios.

The purée can be stored in an airtight container in the refrigerator for up to a week.

BLUEBERRY & OAT MUFFINS

These moist muffins are ideal for breakfast or a mid-morning snack – they'll keep you going for hours.

Preparation time: 15 minutes
Cooking time: 20–25 minutes
Makes 12

....

125 g (4 oz) **wholemeal flour**
125 g (4 oz) **porridge oats**
3 tsps **baking powder**
pinch of **salt**
1 tsp **ground cinnamon**,
    plus extra for dusting
125 g (4 oz) light soft **brown sugar**
finely grated rind of ½ **lemon**
finely grated rind of ½ **orange**
1 large **egg**
100 ml (3½ fl oz) **live natural yogurt**
100 ml (3½ fl oz) **whole milk**
    or **lactose-free milk**
50 g (2 oz) **unsalted butter**, melted
200 g (7 oz) fresh or frozen **blueberries**

Place the flour, oats, baking powder, salt, cinnamon, sugar, orange rind and lemon rind in a large bowl and stir until well combined. In a separate bowl, beat together the egg, yogurt, milk and melted butter and fold gently and quickly into the dry ingredients, mixing until only just combined.

....

Gently stir the blueberries into the muffin mixture and spoon into a 12-hole muffin tin lined with paper cases. Dust each muffin with a little extra cinnamon.

....

Place in a preheated oven, 200°C (400°F), Gas Mark 6, for 20–25 minutes, or until golden and risen. Remove from the tin and cool on a wire rack. Store in an airtight container for up to 4 days.

....

QUINOA PORRIDGE WITH POMEGRANATE

Quinoa, rich in key amino acids and other nutrients, makes a nutritious, filling and mood-lifting breakfast.

Preparation time: 10 minutes
Cooking time: 25 minutes
Serves 4

....

300 g (10 oz) **quinoa**
600 ml (1 pint) **skimmed milk**
    or **lactose-free milk**, plus extra to serve
4 tbsps unsweetened **pomegranate juice**
1 tsp **honey**
seeds from 1 **pomegranate**

Place the quinoa and milk in a large nonstick saucepan over a medium heat and bring to the boil. Reduce the heat to a slow simmer and cook for 20 minutes, or until the milk has been absorbed and the quinoa seeds are plump. Stir frequently and top up with a little more milk or water if it becomes too dry.

....

Meanwhile, mix the pomegranate juice and honey in a small bowl and add the pomegranate seeds.

....

Divide the porridge between 4 serving bowls, top with the pomegranate mixture and serve with a little extra milk.

....

BREAKFAST CEREAL BARS

Packed with seeds, nuts and wholegrains, these nutritious bars are perfect for breakfast on the run.

Preparation time: 10 minutes, plus cooling
Cooking time: 35 minutes
Makes 16

....

100 g (3½ oz) **butter**, softened
25 g (1 oz) light soft **brown sugar**
2 tbsps **golden syrup**
125 g (4 oz) **millet flakes**
50 g (2 oz) **quinoa**
50 g (2 oz) **dried cherries** or **cranberries**
75 g (3 oz) **sultanas**
25 g (1 oz) **sunflower seeds**
25 g (1 oz) **sesame seeds**
25 g (1 oz) **linseeds**
40 g (1½ oz) unsweetened **desiccated coconut**
2 **eggs**, lightly beaten

Beat the butter, sugar and syrup in a mixing bowl with a wooden spoon until pale and creamy. Add all the remaining ingredients and beat well until combined.

Transfer to a greased 28 x 20 cm (11 x 8 inch) baking tin and level the surface with the back of a spoon. Place in a preheated oven, 180°C (350°F), Gas Mark 4, for 35 minutes until deep golden. Leave to cool in the tin.

Turn out on to a wooden board and carefully cut into 16 fingers using a serrated knife. Store in an airtight container for up to a week.

TURKISH POACHED EGGS WITH YOGURT

Ideal for a lazy weekend breakfast, these delicious poached eggs can also be served with salad for a light lunch.

Preparation time: 10 minutes
Cooking time: 10 minutes
Serves 4

4 large **eggs**
3 tbsps **vinegar**
250 ml (8 fl oz) **live natural yogurt**
1 garlic **clove**, crushed
2 tsps **paprika**
1 tbsp **butter**, melted
1 tbsp finely chopped dried or fresh **mint**
sea salt and **black pepper**

Bring a saucepan of water to the boil, add the vinegar and reduce the heat to a slow simmer. One by one, crack the eggs into the water and cook for 3-4 minutes, or until the whites are firm but the yolks still runny.

Meanwhile, mix the yogurt and garlic and season to taste. Divide the yogurt between 4 serving plates, and spread into a circle. In a separate small bowl, mix together the paprika and butter.

Remove the eggs from the pan with a slotted spoon and arrange on top of the yogurt on the plates. Drizzle with the paprika butter and sprinkle with mint. Serve immediately.

SCRAMBLED EGGS ON GRILLED MUSHROOMS

Creamy scrambled eggs, served on portabella mushrooms, lift the mood and provide a filling start to the day.

Preparation time: 15 minutes
Cooking time: 10 minutes
Serves 4

4 large **portabella mushrooms**, stalks removed
1 tsp **olive oil**
½ tsp **dried thyme**
6 **eggs**, beaten
2 tbsps **live natural yogurt**
1 tsp chopped **chives**
1 tsp chopped **dill**
sea salt and **black pepper**

Drizzle the mushrooms with the olive oil, sprinkle with the thyme and season to taste. Cook under a preheated hot grill for 8 minutes until tender, turning once.

Meanwhile, place the eggs, yogurt, chives and dill in a mixing bowl, season to taste and beat until smooth. Heat a nonstick saucepan over a medium heat and add the egg mixture. Stir constantly until the eggs are smooth, creamy and just beginning to set.

Transfer the mushrooms to serving plates and top with the scrambled eggs. Season with black pepper and serve immediately.

BACON & MUSHROOM FRITTATA

This is a healthy version of the English breakfast, with a good boost of B vitamins to support the nervous system.

Preparation time: 10 minutes, plus cooling
Cooking time: 25–30 minutes
Serves 4
....

8 large **chestnut mushrooms**
1 garlic **clove**, finely chopped (optional)
olive oil spray
4 lean **smoked back bacon rashers**
6 large **eggs**
1 tbsp chopped **chives**, plus extra to garnish
1 tbsp **wholegrain mustard**
knob of **butter**
4 large slices of **wholegrain bread**, toasted
sea salt and **black pepper**

Place the mushrooms on a foil-lined baking sheet and scatter over the garlic, if using. Spray with a little olive oil, season to taste and place in a preheated oven, 180°C (350°F), Gas Mark 4, for 18–20 minutes or until tender. Leave until cool enough to handle.

....

Meanwhile, lay the bacon rashers on a foil-lined grill pan and cook under a preheated medium-hot grill for 5–6 minutes, turning once, or until slightly crispy. Leave until cool enough to handle, then slice thickly.

....

Place the eggs, chives and mustard in a bowl, beat together lightly and season to taste. Heat a large nonstick ovenproof frying pan over a medium heat, add the butter and heat until beginning to froth. Pour in the egg mixture and cook for 1–2 minutes, then add the bacon and whole mushrooms, stalk sides up. Cook for a further 2–3 minutes or until almost set.

....

Place the pan under a preheated hot grill and cook for a further 2–3 minutes until set. Cut the frittata into wedges and serve on the toast, garnished with chives.

....

HERBY SMOKED SALMON OMELETTE

The omega oils in salmon are good for the heart and brain, so choose this breakfast when you need to run on all cylinders.

Preparation time: 10 minutes
Cooking time: 15 minutes
Serves 4

8 large **eggs**
2 **spring onions**, thinly sliced
2 tbsps chopped **chives**
2 tbsps chopped **chervil**
50 g (2 oz) **butter**
125 g (4 oz) **smoked salmon**, cut into thin strips
black pepper
baby leaf and herb salad, to serve

Place the eggs, spring onions and herbs in a bowl, beat together lightly and season with pepper.

Heat a frying pan over a medium-low heat, add one-quarter of the butter and melt until beginning to froth. Pour in one-quarter of the egg mixture and swirl to cover the base of the pan. Stir gently for 2–3 minutes or until almost set.

Sprinkle over one-quarter of the smoked salmon and cook for a further 30 seconds or until just set. Fold the omelette in half and slide on to a warmed serving plate.

Repeat with the remaining ingredients to make 3 more omelettes and serve immediately with a baby leaf and herb salad.

SALMON & ASPARAGUS ROLL-UPS

Prepare a few of these tasty little snacks in advance and wrap individually for an instant energy boost.

Preparation time: 10 minutes
Cooking time: 5 minutes
Serves 4

....

4 large or 8 medium **asparagus spears**
4 slices of **smoked salmon**
2 tsps **half-fat cream cheese**
1 tsp chopped **dill**
finely grated rind of ½ **lemon**
black pepper

Break the woody ends off the asparagus spears, then cook in a saucepan of lightly salted boiling water for about 4 minutes until just tender. Drain and plunge into a bowl of cold water to refresh.

....

Meanwhile, mix together the cream cheese, dill, lemon rind and black pepper and spread the mixture on the smoked salmon slices. When the asparagus is cool, place one large spear or two medium spears at the end of each smoked salmon slice and roll up tightly.

....

TZATZIKI WITH RYE TOAST

Tzatziki is a nutritious, low-fat dip which can be served with fresh crudités or, in this case, crunchy rye toast.

Preparation time: 15 minutes, plus standing
Cooking time: 5 minutes
Serves 4

3 **garlic cloves**, crushed
75 g (3 oz) **dill**, finely chopped
75 g (3 oz) **mint**, finely chopped
75 g (3 oz) fresh **coriander**, finely chopped
½ **cucumber**, deseeded and finely chopped
1 small **red chilli**, deseeded
  and finely chopped
600 ml (1 pint) **live Greek yogurt**
sea salt and **black pepper**
100 per cent **rye bread**, to serve

Place all the ingredients in a blender or food processor and blend until smooth. Season to taste then set aside for at least 1 hour before serving to allow the flavours to mingle.

Thinly slice the rye bread and toast until crisp and lightly browned. Serve with the tzatziki on top. The tzatziki can be kept in an airtight container in the refrigerator for up to 4 days. Stir well before serving.

BLACK OLIVE
TAPENADE WITH OATCAKES

Olives prevent cholesterol build-up in the arteries,
and anchovies provide brain-nourishing omega-3 oils.

Preparation time: 5 minutes
Serves 4

3 tsps **capers**, rinsed and drained
4 canned **anchovy fillets**
1 **garlic clove**, crushed
finely grated rind and juice of 1 **lemon**
250 g (8 oz) pitted **black olives**
2 tsps chopped **parsley**
3–4 tsps **olive oil**
sea salt and **black pepper**
oatcakes or toasted **wholegrain
    pitta breads**, to serve

Place the capers, anchovy fillets, garlic,
lemon rind and lemon juice in a blender
or food processor and blend for about
10 seconds, until you have a rough purée.

Add the olives, parsley and enough olive
 oil to make a paste. Blitz again then season
to taste. Serve with oatcakes or toasted
wholegrain pitta breads.

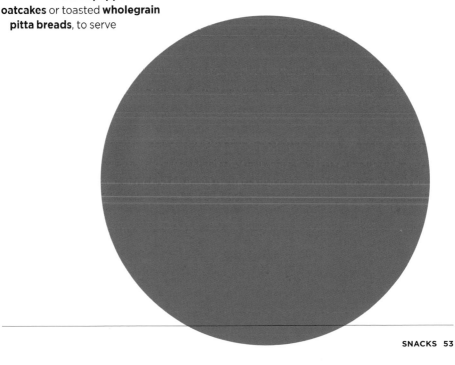

GUACAMOLE WITH TORTILLA BITES

This is an easy snack or side dish for a Mexican-style feast. The avocados are not just filling, but hugely nutritious.

Preparation time: 10 minutes
Cooking time: 15 minutes
Serves 4

4 wholegrain soft flour **tortillas**
1 tsp **olive oil**
1 tsp **paprika**
3 large, ripe **avocados**, peeled and stoned
3 **spring onions**, finely chopped
1 large ripe **tomato**, finely chopped
75 g (3 oz) fresh **coriander**, finely chopped
finely grated rind and juice of 1 **lime**
2 **garlic cloves**, crushed

Brush the tortillas on both sides with the olive oil and cut into triangles, roughly the shape of shop-bought tortilla chips. Transfer to a baking sheet, sprinkle with paprika and place in a preheated oven, 200°C (400°F), Gas Mark 6, for 10 minutes until crisp.

Meanwhile, place the avocado in a bowl and mash with the onions, tomato, coriander, lime rind and juice and garlic until smooth. Serve with the tortilla bites.

Any leftover guacamole can be stored in an airtight container in the refrigerator with the stone of the avocado, which helps to prevent browning, for up to 2 days.

GARLIC & FLAGEOLET BEAN PÂTÉ

Immune-boosting, blood-cleansing garlic accompanies rich pesto and energy-sustaining pulses in this tasty dip.

Preparation time: 10 minutes
Serves 4

....

400 g (13 oz) can **flageolet beans**, rinsed and drained
125 g (4 oz) **cream cheese**
2 **garlic cloves**, chopped
3 tsps ready-made **pesto**
2 **spring onions**, chopped
1 tsp **olive oil**
sea salt and **black pepper**

To serve
cucumber sticks
4 **wholemeal pitta breads**

Place the beans, cream cheese, garlic and 2 tsps of the pesto in a blender or food processor and blend until smooth. Add the spring onions, season to taste and blend for a further 10 seconds. Spoon into a dish and chill until required.

....

Mix the remaining pesto with the olive oil and drizzle over the pâté before serving with cucumber sticks and fingers of lightly toasted pitta bread.

....

Any leftover pâté can be stored in an airtight container in the refrigerator for up to 4 days.

....

AVOCADO WITH YOGURT DRESSING

Avocados, bursting with beneficial fats, are here served with a yogurt dressing as a quick snack or side dish.

Preparation time: 15 minutes
Serves 4
....

2 ripe **avocados**, peeled, stoned and sliced
1 tsp **lemon juice**

Dressing
125 ml (4 fl oz) **low-fat live natural yogurt**
4 tsps chopped fresh **coriander**
1 tsp chopped **mint**
½ small **red onion**, finely chopped
1 **garlic clove**, finely chopped
1 tsp **lemon juice**
finely grated rind of ½ **lemon**

Toss the avocado slices with the lemon juice and arrange on serving plates. Place all the dressing ingredients in a blender or food processor and blend until smooth. Drizzle over the avocado and serve immediately.
....

Any leftover dressing can be stored in an airtight container in the refrigerator for up to 2 days.
....

EDAMAME BEAN HUMMUS

Edamame beans (soya) balance hormones and are a good source of protein. Serve this hummus with wholemeal toast, crudités or seedy breadsticks.

Preparation time: 10 minutes
Cooking time: 4 minutes
Serves 4

250 g (8 oz) frozen **edamame beans**
50 g (2 oz) **tahini**
½ tsp finely grated **lemon** rind
4 tsps **lemon juice**
1 **garlic clove**, crushed
1 **spring onion**, finely chopped
¾ tsp **sea salt**
½ tsp **ground cumin**
½ tsp **ground coriander**
pinch of **ground cinnamon**
3 tsps **olive oil**
2 tsps chopped fresh **coriander**

Cook the beans in a saucepan of lightly salted boiling water for 3–4 minutes, until just tender. Drain and place in a blender or food processor with the tahini, lemon rind and juice, garlic, spring onion, salt and spices and blend until smooth.

With the motor still running, slowly pour in the olive oil until the hummus has emulsified. Transfer to a serving dish and sprinkle with the chopped coriander.

Any leftover hummus can be stored in an airtight container in the refrigerator for up to 4 days.

STUFFED EGGS

These herby eggs will appeal to the whole family and provide calming nutrients at the same time.

Preparation time: 15 minutes
Serves 4
....

4 hard-boiled **eggs**, shelled
2 tsps **live natural yogurt**
1 tsp finely chopped **chives**
1 tsp finely chopped **dill**
½ tsp finely chopped **tarragon**
1 tsp finely grated **lemon** rind
sea salt and **black pepper**

Cut the eggs in half lengthways and remove the yolks. Place the yolks in a small bowl with the remaining ingredients, season to taste and mash to combine.
....

Arrange the whites, cut sides up, on a serving plate. Carefully spoon the yolk mixture back into the hollows and serve immediately.
....

APRICOT, MANGO & PINEAPPLE SMOOTHIE

This energy-boosting smoothie combines immune-boosting apricot and mango with digestion-soothing pineapple.

Preparation time: 10 minutes, plus soaking and freezing
Serves 4
....

3 ripe **mangoes**, peeled, stoned, and roughly chopped
75 g (3 oz) soft **dried apricots**
600 ml (1 pint) **pineapple juice**
1 **pineapple**, peeled, cored and chopped
finely grated rind and juice of 2 **limes**

Place the mango chunks in a freezer container and freeze overnight. Place the apricots in a bowl with the pineapple juice and chill overnight.

....

The next morning, place all the ingredients in a blender or food processor and blend until smooth. Serve immediately.

....

CHOCOLATE & ALMOND SQUARES

With fewer than 200 calories each, these satisfying snacks are full of stress-busting wholegrains, nuts and seeds.

Preparation time: 10 minutes,
   plus cooling and chilling
Cooking time: 20 minutes
Makes 15-20

....

finely grated rind of 1 **lemon**
75 g (3 oz) soft **dried dates**, chopped
100 g (3½ oz) **almonds**, chopped
125 g (4 oz) light soft **brown sugar**
150 g (5 oz) **millet flakes**
40 g (1½ oz) **cornflakes**, lightly crushed
65 g (2½ oz) **bran flakes**
400 g (13 oz) can **condensed milk**
50 g (2 oz) **plain chocolate**, melted,
   plus extra to drizzle (optional)
25 g (1 oz) **mixed seeds**, such as pumpkin,
   sesame and sunflower

Place all the ingredients in a large bowl and mix together. Spoon into a 28 x 18 cm (11 x 7 inch) nonstick baking tin and place in a preheated oven, 180°C (350°F), Gas Mark 4, for 20 minutes.

....

Remove from the oven and allow to cool. Once cool, drizzle the top with melted chocolate, if liked. Mark into 15–20 squares and chill in the refrigerator until firm. Store in an airtight container in a cool place for up to a week.

....

FRUITY MANGO FLAPJACKS

Flapjacks are the perfect snack, providing slow-release energy and keeping stress and all of its symptoms at bay.

Preparation time: 10 minutes, plus cooling
Cooking time: 30 minutes
Makes 12

....

100 g (3½ oz) light soft **brown sugar**
150 g (5 oz) **butter**
2 tsps **golden syrup**
200 g (7 oz) **porridge oats**
4 tsps **mixed seeds**, such as pumpkin
    and sunflower
75 g (3 oz) **dried mango**, roughly chopped

Place the sugar, butter and syrup in a large, heavy-based saucepan over a low heat until melted, then remove from the heat and stir in the remaining ingredients.

....

Spoon the mixture into a 28 x 18 cm (11 x 7 inch) nonstick baking tin, press down lightly and place in a preheated oven, 150°C (300°F), Gas Mark 2, for 30 minutes until golden round the edges.

....

Use a small knife to score the flapjack into 12 pieces, then allow to cool completely before removing from the tin. Cut or break into 12 pieces once cooled. Store in an airtight container for up to a week.

....

SWEET POTATO & CABBAGE SOUP

Full of fibre and antioxidants to protect against the effects of stress, this soup is also hearty and flavoursome.

Preparation time: 20 minutes
Cooking time: 25 minutes
Serves 4

2 **onions**, chopped
2 **garlic cloves**, sliced
4 **back bacon** or **turkey bacon**
  rashers, chopped
500 g (1 lb) **sweet potatoes**,
  peeled and chopped
2 **parsnips**, chopped
1 tsp chopped **thyme**
900 ml (1½ pints) **vegetable stock**
1 baby **Savoy cabbage**, shredded
sea salt and **black pepper**
soda bread, to serve

Place the onions, garlic and bacon in a large saucepan over a medium heat and cook for 2–3 minutes. Add the sweet potatoes, parsnips, thyme and stock, bring to the boil and simmer for 15 minutes or until the vegetables are tender.

Remove from the heat, allow to cool slightly, then transfer two-thirds of the soup to a blender or food processor and blend until smooth. Return to the pan, add the cabbage and continue to simmer for 5–7 minutes until the cabbage is just cooked. Season to taste, ladle the soup into warmed bowls and serve with soda bread.

BACON & CANNELLINI BEAN SOUP

A filling winter soup bursting with warming flavours and low-GI pulses to keep energy levels steady.

Preparation time: 15 minutes
Cooking time: 20 minutes
Serves 4

1 tsp **olive oil**
2 **smoked bacon rashers**, chopped
2 **garlic cloves**, crushed
1 **celery stick**, finely chopped
1 **carrot**, finely chopped
1 **onion**, chopped
2 tsps **dried thyme**
finely grated rind and juice of 1 **lemon**
2 x 400 g (13 oz) cans **cannellini beans**, drained and rinsed
900 ml (1½ pints) **vegetable stock**
2 tbsps chopped **parsley**
sea salt and **black pepper**
crusty **bread**, to serve

Heat the oil in a large saucepan, add the bacon, garlic, celery, carrot and onion and cook over a medium heat for 3–4 minutes until the bacon is beginning to brown and the onion soften.

Add the thyme, lemon juice and lemon rind and continue to cook for 1 minute. Add the beans and stock to the pan, bring to the boil, reduce the heat and simmer for 10 minutes.

Remove from the heat, allow to cool slightly, then transfer the soup to a blender or food processor and blend with the parsley until smooth. Return to the pan, season to taste and heat through. Ladle the soup into warmed bowls and serve with crusty bread.

GRILLED MUSHROOM & GARLIC WRAPS

Mushrooms are a key calming ingredient, encouraging healthy sleep and reducing the effects of stress on mind and body.

Preparation time: 20 minutes
Cooking time: 15 minutes
Serves 4

················

500 g (1 lb) large **field mushrooms**, thickly sliced
2 **garlic cloves**, finely chopped
3 **spring onions**, thinly sliced
2 tbsps **olive oil**
100 g (3½ oz) **cream cheese**
4 large wholegrain soft flour **tortillas**
4 tbsps chopped **chives**
12 **cherry tomatoes**, quartered
2 **romaine lettuces**, shredded
sea salt and **black pepper**

Toss the mushrooms with the garlic, spring onions and olive oil in a large bowl. Season to taste, tip on to a nonstick baking sheet and place under a preheated medium grill for 6–8 minutes until tender, turning frequently.

····················

Meanwhile, spread the cream cheese over the tortilla wraps and scatter over the chives. Divide the mushrooms between the wraps, scatter over the cherry tomatoes and top with a handful of the lettuce. Fold up the tortillas to completely enclose the filling, creating 4 parcels.

····································

Heat a large, ridged griddle pan over a medium-high heat. Place the parcels on the griddle and toast for 4–5 minutes, turning occasionally, until nicely charred on both sides. This may need to be done in two batches. Cut in half and serve immediately with the remaining lettuce.

····································

LEMONY SCALLOP SKEWERS WITH ROCKET

Treat yourself to this simple, elegant lunch for a special occasion and boost your immunity at the same time.

Preparation time: 10 minutes
Cooking time: 5 minutes
Serves 4
....

400 g (13 oz) **queen scallops** without roes
finely grated rind and juice of 1 **lemon**
3 tsps **basil oil**
75 g (3 oz) blanched **hazelnuts**
200 g (7 oz) **wild rocket**
sea salt and **black pepper**

Place the scallops in a bowl with the lemon rind and 2 tsps of the basil oil and season with pepper. Mix well to coat, then thread the scallops on to 4 metal skewers.

Place the skewers under a preheated hot grill for 2–3 minutes until just cooked, turning occasionally. They are ready as soon as they are firm and opaque.

Meanwhile, heat a small frying pan over a medium heat, tip in the hazelnuts and dry-roast until golden, shaking the pan frequently. Tip the nuts into a small dish and crush lightly.

Toss the rocket leaves with the remaining basil oil and the lemon juice and season to taste. Arrange on 4 serving plates and top with the scallop skewers. Scatter over the hazelnuts and serve immediately.

PUY LENTILS WITH FLAKED SALMON

This powerful stress-busting combination of lentils and salmon will encourage relaxation and wellbeing on all levels.

Preparation time: 30 minutes
Cooking time: 25 minutes
Serves 4

500 g (1 lb) **salmon tail fillet**
2 tbsps dry **white wine**
125 g (4 oz) **Puy lentils**, well rinsed
2 **red peppers**, halved, cored and deseeded
large handful of **dill**, chopped
finely grated rind and juice of 1 **lemon**
bunch of **spring onions**, finely sliced
sea salt and **black pepper**

Dressing
2 **garlic cloves**
large handful of **flat leaf parsley**, chopped
large handful of **dill**, chopped
1 tsp **Dijon mustard**
2 **green chillies**, deseeded and chopped
juice of 2 large **lemons**
1 tbsp **olive oil**

Place the salmon on a large sheet of foil and spoon over the wine. Gather up the sides of the foil and fold over at the top to seal into a parcel. Place on a baking sheet and bake in a preheated oven, 200°C (400°F), Gas Mark 6, for 15–20 minutes until just cooked.

Place the lentils in a large saucepan with plenty of water, bring to the boil, then simmer gently for about 15–20 minutes until cooked but still firm to the bite.

Meanwhile, place the peppers skin-side up under a preheated hot grill until charred. Place in a plastic bag for a few minutes. Remove from the bag, peel off the skin and cut the flesh into 2.5 cm (1 inch) squares.

Place all the dressing ingredients, except the oil, in a blender or food processor and blend until smooth. With the motor still running, drizzle in the oil until the mixture is thick. Season to taste.

Drain the lentils and place in a bowl with the red pepper, dill, lemon rind and most of the spring onions. Season to taste and stir in the dressing. Flake the salmon and gently stir through the lentils. Squeeze over lemon juice to taste and scatter with the remaining spring onions. Serve warm or cold.

SMOKED MACKEREL PASTA SALAD

Smoked mackerel is the ultimate in convenience superfoods and provides a heart-healthy, nervous-system boosting meal in moments.

Preparation time: 15 minutes
Cooking time: 10–15 minutes
Serves 4

300 g (10 oz) **wholegrain** or spelt **conchiglie pasta**
200 g (7 oz) **green beans**, trimmed
4 **pepper-crusted smoked mackerel fillets**, skin and bones removed
125 g (4 oz) **mixed peppery salad leaves**
½ **cucumber**, deseeded and chopped
2 **spring onions**, finely sliced
2 hard-boiled **eggs**, shelled and quartered

Dressing
100 ml (3½ fl oz) **half-fat soured cream**
1 tbsp **wholegrain mustard**
1 tsp **French mustard**
2 tbsps **lemon juice**
1 tsp chopped **dill**
1 tsp chopped **tarragon**
sea salt and **black pepper**

Cook the pasta in a large saucepan of lightly salted boiling water for 11 minutes or until al dente. Drain and cool under cold running water. Tip into a large bowl and set aside.

Meanwhile, cook the beans in a saucepan of lightly salted boiling water for 4–5 minutes until just tender. Drain and cool under cold running water, then add to the bowl with the pasta.

Place all the dressing ingredients in a screw-top jar, season to taste and shake vigorously until well combined.

Flake the smoked mackerel into large pieces and stir into the pasta and beans with the salad leaves, cucumber and spring onions. Toss with a little of the dressing and divide between 4 serving bowls. Top with the hard-boiled eggs and serve with the remaining dressing on the side.

ROASTED BEETROOT & FETA SALAD WITH ALMONDS

Beetroot provides a powerhouse of nutrients and this warm, tasty salad will lift the mood and keep you satisfied for hours.

Preparation time: 20 minutes
Cooking time: 25 minutes
Serves 4

8 large **beetroot**, peeled
   and cut into chunks
2 tbsps **olive oil**
50 g (2 oz) blanched **almonds**
100 g (3½ oz) **rocket**
150 g (5 oz) **feta cheese**
2 tbsps **balsamic** glaze
4–5 **mint leaves**, chopped
sea salt and **black pepper**

Place the beetroot on a nonstick baking sheet and drizzle with the olive oil. Season to taste and use your hands to toss the beetroot in the oil until evenly coated.

Place in a preheated oven, 200°C (400°F), Gas Mark 6, for about 25 minutes until tender, turning once or twice. About 5 minutes before the end of cooking time, add the almonds to the tray.

Divide the rocket between 4 serving plates, top with the beetroot and almonds and crumble the feta cheese over the top. Drizzle with the balsamic glaze and the oil from the baking sheet.

Sprinkle with the mint and serve warm or cold. The salad can be stored in an airtight container in the refrigerator for up to 2 days.

GOATS' CHEESE, APPLE & WALNUT SALAD

This fruity, filling salad is rich in protein and antioxidant nutrients to help prevent damage caused by stress.

Preparation time: 15 minutes
Cooking time: 5 minutes
Serves 4
....

2 **goats' cheese** logs, cut
   into 1 cm (½ inch) slices
2 tsps **olive oil**
200 g (7 oz) **mixed salad leaves**
16 soft **dried apricots**, sliced
100 g (3½ oz) **walnuts**, lightly toasted
handful of **grapes**, halved
2 **Granny Smith apples**, peeled,
   cored and cut into slices
sea salt and **black pepper**
wholegrain rolls, to serve

Dressing
2 tbsps **olive oil**
2 tbsps **lemon juice**
½ tsp **sea salt**
½ tsp **black pepper**
1 tsp **honey**
1 tsp **wholegrain mustard**

Place the goats' cheese slices on a nonstick baking sheet and brush with a little olive oil. Season to taste then place under a medium-hot grill until bubbling. Meanwhile, place all the dressing ingredients in a screw-top jar and shake vigorously until combined.

Divide the salad leaves among 4 plates and top with the apricots, walnuts, grapes and apples. Arrange a hot goats' cheese slice on top of each one and drizzle with the dressing. Serve immediately with wholegrain rolls.

WATERMELON & FETA SALAD

Watermelon is hydrating and a natural source of electrolytes, which boost energy and ease headaches and muscular tension.

Preparation time: 10 minutes
Cooking time: 2 minutes
Serves 4
....

1 tbsp **black sesame seeds**
500 g (1 lb) **watermelon**, peeled, deseeded and diced
175 g (6 oz) **feta cheese**, diced
300 g (10 oz) **rocket**
large handful of **mint, parsley** and **coriander** sprigs
6 tbsps **olive oil**
1 tbsp **orange flower water**
1½ tbsps **lemon juice**
½ tsp **caster sugar**
1 tsp **pomegranate syrup** (optional)
sea salt and **black pepper**

Heat a frying pan and dry-fry the sesame seeds for 2 minutes until aromatic, then set aside. Arrange the watermelon and feta on a large plate with the rocket and herbs.
....

Whisk together the oil, orange flower water, lemon juice, sugar and pomegranate syrup, if using. Season to taste, then drizzle over the salad. Sprinkle with the sesame seeds and serve.
....

WARM SPINACH SALAD

Full of stress-busting superfoods, this salad is ideal for lunch or as a starter or side dish for dinner.

Preparation time: 15 minutes
Cooking time: 10 minutes
Serves 4

1 tsp **olive oil**
4 **unsmoked turkey bacon rashers**
1 **garlic clove**, crushed
1 **shallot**, finely chopped
3 tbsps **sherry vinegar**
1 kg (2 lbs) **spinach**, washed and dried
4 hard-boiled **eggs**, shelled and sliced
8 large **mushrooms**, thinly sliced
1 **avocado**, peeled, stoned and diced
sea salt and **black pepper**

Heat the olive oil in a large nonstick frying pan and add the bacon. Fry until crisp, then remove with a slotted spoon and drain on kitchen paper. Add the garlic and shallot to the pan and sauté very gently for 3–4 minutes.

Stir in the vinegar and season to taste. Turn off the heat and tip in the spinach. Toss it gently in the dressing until just covered and beginning to wilt. Divide the spinach between 4 serving plates and top with the eggs, mushrooms, bacon and avocado. Serve immediately.

GINGERED TOFU & MANGO SALAD

Soya is a good hormone balancer and source of energy. Here it is combined with stress-busting mango.

Preparation time: 15 minutes
Cooking time: 5 minutes
Serves 4

....

250 g (8 oz) **tofu**
50 g (2 oz) fresh **root ginger**, peeled and grated
4 tbsps **light soy sauce**
2 **garlic cloves**, crushed
2 tbsps seasoned **rice vinegar**
4 tbsps **groundnut oil**
2 bunches of **spring onions**, diagonally sliced
100 g (3½ oz) **cashew nuts**
2 small **mangoes**, peeled, stoned and sliced
1 small **iceberg lettuce**, shredded
4 tbsps **water**

Pat the tofu dry on kitchen paper and cut into 1 cm (½ inch) cubes. Mix the ginger, soy sauce, garlic and vinegar in a bowl, add the tofu and toss to coat. Set aside to marinate for 15 minutes.

Remove the tofu from the marinade and reserve the marinade. Heat the oil in a frying pan over a medium heat, add the tofu and cook gently for about 3 minutes until golden. Remove from the pan and keep warm.

Add the spring onions and cashews to the pan and fry quickly for 30 seconds. Add the mango slices and cook for 30 seconds more, until heated through.

Pile the lettuce on to serving plates and scatter the tofu, spring onions, mango and cashews over the top. Heat the marinade juices in the pan with the measurement water, pour the mixture over the salad and serve immediately.

MEDITERRANEAN BROWN RICE SALAD

The vibrant colours pay tribute to the antioxidants in this salad. Add crumbled feta or a few pine nuts before serving if you like.

Preparation time: 25 minutes
Cooking time: 30–40 minutes
Serves 4

....

2 **red peppers**, cored, deseeded and chopped
2 **yellow peppers**, cored, deseeded and chopped
2 large **courgettes**, cubed
4 small **beetroot**, peeled and cubed
1 large **aubergine**, cubed
1 large **onion**, roughly chopped
3 tbsps **olive oil**
2 tsps **dried oregano**
750 g (1½ lb) cooked **brown rice**
sea salt and **black pepper**
5 **basil leaves**, torn, to garnish

Dressing
1 tbsp **olive oil**
1 tsp **honey**
1 tsp **mustard powder**
½ tsp **salt**
½ tsp **black pepper**
1 tsp **dried oregano**
2 tbsps **balsamic vinegar**

Arrange the vegetables on 2 nonstick baking sheets and drizzle with the olive oil. Season to taste, sprinkle with the oregano and use your hands to toss the vegetables in the oil until evenly coated.

....

Place in a preheated oven, 200°C (400°F), Gas Mark 6, for 30–40 minutes until tender and just beginning to brown at the edges, turning once or twice.

....

Transfer the vegetables to a serving bowl with a slotted spoon and set aside. Place all the dressing ingredients in a screw-top jar, season to taste, add the oil from the baking sheets and shake vigorously until well combined.

....

Place the cooked rice and dressing in the bowl with the vegetables and toss together until well mixed. Serve warm or cold, garnished with the basil. The salad can be stored in an airtight container in the refrigerator for up to 5 days.

....

TURKEY, PEANUT & MANGO SALAD

This is a wonderfully fragrant, nutritious lunch. Use the freshest mango you can find for optimum antioxidant protection.

Preparation time: 15 minutes
Serves 4
....

400 g (13 oz) **mixed salad leaves**
500 g (1 lb) cooked **turkey** or **chicken**,
    light and dark meat
200 g (7 oz) **cherry tomatoes,** halved
1 **mango**, peeled, stoned & cut into chunks
100 g (3½ oz) roasted **peanuts**
75 g (3 oz) fresh **coriander**, chopped

Dressing
3 tbsps **olive oil**
2 tbsps **lime juice**
finely grated rind of ½ **lime**
2 tsps **brown sugar**
2 tsps **Thai fish sauce**
½ tsp **sweet chilli sauce**

Place the salad leaves on a large platter and arrange the turkey, cherry tomatoes and mango on top. Sprinkle with the roasted peanuts and coriander.
....

Place all the dressing ingredients in a screw-top jar and shake vigorously until well combined. Pour over the salad, lightly toss and serve.
....

WILD RICE & TURKEY SALAD

Wild rice isn't a rice at all, but a hearty, wholesome grain that has all the benefits of wholegrains.

Preparation time: 10 minutes, plus cooling
Cooking time: 30 minutes
Serves 4
....

300 g (10 oz) **wild rice**
2 **green apples**, quartered,
    cored and finely sliced
75 g (3 oz) **pecan nuts**
finely grated rind and juice of 2 **oranges**
60 g (2¼ oz) **cranberries**
3 tbsps **olive oil**
2 tbsps chopped **parsley**
4 **turkey breast fillets**, about 125 g
    (4 oz) each
sea salt and **black pepper**

Cook the rice according to packet instructions and allow to cool. Mix the apples into the rice with the pecans, orange rind and juice and the cranberries. Season to taste.

....

Mix together the oil and parsley and season to taste. Cut the turkey fillets into halves or thirds lengthways and coat with this mixture.

....

Heat a frying pan until it is hot but not smoking and cook the turkey for 2 minutes on each side until cooked through. Slice the turkey and serve immediately with the rice salad.

....

TURKEY CROQUE MADAME

The tryptophan-rich turkey in this lower-calorie croque madame encourages relaxation, while the spinach balances energy levels.

Preparation time: 10 minutes
Cooking time: 8–10 minutes
Serves 4

8 slices of **wholegrain bread**
3 tbsps **wholegrain mustard**
200 g (7 oz) finely grated **mature Gruyère**
or **reduced-fat Cheddar cheese**,
200 g (7 oz) cooked **turkey**, thinly sliced
2 **tomatoes**, sliced
2 **spring onions**, thinly sliced
4 tbsps **low-fat cream cheese** (optional)
1 tbsp **vinegar**
4 large **eggs**
100 g (3½ oz) **baby leaf spinach**
sea salt and **black pepper**
chopped **chives**, to garnish

Lay 4 slices of the bread on a board and spread with the mustard. Top with half the grated cheese, the turkey and tomato slices, then scatter with the spring onions. Season to taste and scatter over the remaining grated cheese.

Spread the cream cheese, if using, over the remaining slices of bread and place, cheese-side down, on top of the sandwiches.

Heat a large, nonstick frying pan over a medium heat until hot, then carefully add the sandwiches and cook for 4–5 minutes or until golden and crispy. This may need to be done in two batches. Turn the sandwiches over and cook for a further 4–5 minutes.

Meanwhile, bring a large saucepan of water to a gentle simmer and add the vinegar. Carefully break 2 eggs into the water and cook for 3 minutes. Remove with a slotted spoon and keep warm. Repeat with the remaining eggs.

Place the sandwiches on serving plates, scatter with the spinach leaves and top each with a poached egg. Garnish with chives and serve immediately.

FISH & MANGO CURRY WITH BROWN RICE

This Thai-inspired dish is quick and nutritious. Use haddock, halibut or coley – or chicken or king prawns if you prefer.

Preparation time: 20 minutes
Cooking time: 20 minutes
Serves 4

....

2 tbsps **olive oil**
2 x 400 ml (14 fl oz) cans **coconut milk**
750 g (1½ lb) firm **white fish fillets**,
   cut into chunks
1 large **mango**, peeled and cut into chunks

Curry paste
5 cm (2 in) piece of fresh **root ginger**,
   peeled and chopped
finely grated rind and juice of 2 **limes**
2 small **green chillies**, deseeded
3 **lemon grass stalks**, outer leaves removed
4 **shallots**, peeled
75 g (3 oz) fresh **coriander**
4 **garlic cloves**
1 tsp **sea salt**
3 tbsps **Thai fish sauce**

To serve
brown rice
25 g (1 oz) fresh **coriander**, roughly torn

Place all the curry paste ingredients in a food processor or mini-chopper and blend until smooth, adding a little water if it is too dry to make a paste.

Heat the oil in a nonstick frying pan or wok, add the curry paste and cook gently for 2–3 minutes. Add the coconut milk and cook, covered, for 5 minutes. Add the fish, stir gently, and continue to cook for a further 5 minutes.

Stir in the mango and cook, uncovered, for 3–4 minutes until the fish is flaky and the mango heated through. Serve with brown rice and a generous sprinkling of coriander.

SALMON WITH BEAN & CELERIAC MASH

With omega-rich salmon and high-quality protein in the pulses, this dish will calm, relax and ensure a good night's sleep.

Preparation time: 15 minutes
Cooking time: 20 minutes
Serves 4

250 g (8 oz) **celeriac**, cut into chunks
250 g (8 oz) **potatoes**, cut into chunks
125 g (4 oz) cooked **edamame beans**
3 tbsps **water**
4 **salmon fillets**, about 125 g (4 oz) each
40 g (1½ oz) **butter**
3 tbsps chopped **chives**
3 tbsps chopped **tarragon** or **dill**
1 tbsp **white wine vinegar**
sea salt and **black pepper**

Cook the celeriac and potatoes in a saucepan of lightly salted boiling water for about 15 minutes, until tender. Place the beans and measurement water in a blender or food processor and blend until smooth.

Meanwhile, pat the salmon fillets dry on kitchen paper and season to taste. Heat 15 g (½ oz) of the butter in a frying pan and fry the salmon for 4–5 minutes on each side, until just cooked through.

Drain the vegetables and return them to the pan with the blended beans and a further 15 g (½ oz) of the butter. Using a potato masher, mash the ingredients together until evenly combined. Reheat for 1–2 minutes and season to taste.

Pile the mash on to 4 warmed serving plates and top with the salmon fillets. Add the remaining butter, herbs and vinegar to the frying pan and heat through until the mixture bubbles. Pour the sauce over the salmon and serve immediately.

SPICY PRAWN KEBABS WITH WILD RICE

A great source of zinc for memory, energy and libido, these spicy prawn kebabs are delicious and quick to prepare.

Preparation time: 10 minutes
Cooking time: 5 minutes
Serves 4

....

24 raw peeled **king prawns**
125 ml (4 fl oz) **sweet chilli sauce**
finely grated rind and juice of 2 **limes**
4 tbsps **light soy sauce**
1 tbsp **sesame oil**
sea salt and **black pepper**

To serve
wild rice
crunchy **green salad**

Thread the prawns on to 4 metal skewers, running the skewers through the prawns in 2 or 3 places to secure. Whisk together the chilli sauce, lime rind and juice, soy sauce and sesame oil, and brush on both sizes of the prawns.

....

Place under a preheated hot grill and cook for 1–2 minutes on each side until pink and just cooked through. Serve with wild rice and a crunchy green salad.

....

THAI MUSSEL CURRY WITH GINGER

This fragrant, light curry provides a good boost of zinc, to encourage energy and even support a flagging libido.

Preparation time: 30 minutes
Cooking time: 15 minutes
Serves 4

1.5 kg (3 lb) **mussels**
1 tbsp **sunflower oil**
400 ml (14 fl oz) can **reduced-fat coconut milk**
4–5 **kaffir lime leaves**
150 ml (¼ pint) **fish stock**
2 tsps **Thai fish sauce**

Curry paste
½ –1 large **red chilli**, halved and deseeded
2 **shallots**, peeled
1 **lemon grass stalk**, outer leaves removed
finely grated rind and juice of 1 **lime**
4 cm (1½ inch) piece of fresh **root ginger**, peeled and chopped

To serve
50 g (2 oz) fresh **coriander**, roughly torn
brown rice

To prepare the mussels, remove any barnacles with a small knife and pull off the hairy beards. Rinse the shells well and discard any mussels which are open or have broken shells. Put them in a bowl of clean water until ready to cook.

Place all the curry paste ingredients in a food processor or mini-chopper and blend until smooth, adding a little water if it is too dry to make a paste.

Heat the oil in a nonstick frying pan or wok, add the curry paste and cook gently for 5 minutes. Add the coconut milk, kaffir lime leaves, fish stock and fish sauce and cook for 3 minutes.

Drain the mussels and add to the pan. Cover and cook for about 5 minutes until the mussel shells have opened. Divide between 4 warmed bowls, discarding any mussels that have not opened. Scatter the coriander over the top and serve with brown rice.

ROOT VEGETABLE TAGINE WITH POMEGRANATE SALSA

This fragrant Moroccan tagine contains a medley of stress-busting herbs, spices and root vegetables.

Preparation time: 25 minutes
Cooking time: 1 hour
Serves 6–8

....

1 **cinnamon stick**
½ tsp **cloves**
½ tsp **cardamom seeds**
2 tsps **coriander seeds**
1 tsp **ground turmeric**
1 tbsp **olive oil**
1 large **onion**, chopped
2.5 cm (1 inch) piece of fresh **root ginger**,
   peeled and grated
3 **garlic cloves**, finely chopped
½ **red chilli**, deseeded and chopped
2 x 400 g (13 oz) cans **chopped tomatoes**
1 large **carrot**, cubed
1 **sweet potato**, cubed
½ **butternut squash**, cubed
100 g (3½ oz) **spinach**
400 g (13 oz) can **chickpeas**,
   rinsed and drained
handful of fresh **coriander**, chopped
1 tsp **harissa**
quinoa, to serve

Pomegranate salsa
seeds from 1 **pomegranate**
2 spring **onions**, finely chopped
juice of 1 **lime**
10–12 **mint leaves**, finely chopped
1 tbsp **olive oil**

Dry-fry the cinnamon, cloves, cardamom and coriander seeds in a frying pan until their fragrance is released. Use a mortar and pestle or a clean coffee grinder to grind them to a powder with the turmeric.

....

Heat the olive oil in a large, heavy-based pan and stir in the spices. Add the onion and cook for 2–3 minutes, then add the ginger, garlic and chilli. Reduce the heat and cook gently for 10 minutes until soft.

....

Add the tomatoes, carrot, sweet potatoes and squash, cover and simmer for 30–40 minutes until the vegetables are tender.

....

Stir the spinach, chickpeas, coriander and harissa into the tagine, season to taste with salt and black pepper, cover and set aside.

....

Make the pomegranate salsa by mixing together all the ingredients. Serve the tagine on a bed of quinoa with the salsa on the side.

....

GINGERY CHICKPEA CURRY

This quick curry provides plenty of protein to encourage stable blood sugar levels and promote healing.

Preparation time: 15 minutes
Cooking time: 40 minutes
Serves 4

········

1 tbsp **olive oil**
2 **garlic cloves**, crushed
2 **onions**, chopped
7.5 cm (3 in) piece of fresh **root ginger**,
    grated, plus extra to serve
1 tsp **mild chilli powder**
1 tsp **ground cumin**
½ tsp **ground coriander**
½ tsp **ground turmeric**
½ tsp **sea salt**
½ tsp **garam masala**, plus extra to serve
2 x 400 g (13 oz) cans **chickpeas**,
    rinsed and drained
400 ml (14 fl oz) can **coconut milk**
75 g (3 oz) fresh **coriander**, chopped
black pepper
quinoa or **brown rice**, to serve

Heat the oil in a deep saucepan or wok over a medium heat and add the garlic, onions and ginger. Cook slowly, stirring often, until the onions are soft and beginning to caramelize.

·············

Add the chilli powder, cumin, ground coriander, turmeric, sea salt and garam masala and cook for a further 2–3 minutes. Add the chickpeas and coconut milk, stir well, cover and simmer for 20 minutes.

·············

Remove the lid and continue to cook for another 10 minutes, mashing some of the chickpeas into the sauce to thicken. Season with pepper, sprinkle with a pinch of garam masala, a grating of fresh ginger and the fresh coriander and serve immediately with quinoa or brown rice.

·············

POTATO & ONION TORTILLA

Keep the skin on the potatoes to add extra fibre to this surprisingly light tortilla and add a handful of grated Gruyère if you like.

Preparation time: 10 minutes
Cooking time: 30 minutes
Serves 6

....

750 g (1½ lb) **potatoes**, very thinly sliced
4 tbsps **olive oil**
2 large **onions**, thinly sliced
6 **eggs**
2 tsps **dried thyme**
1 tsp **dried rosemary**
sea salt and **black pepper**

Place the potatoes in a bowl and toss with a little seasoning. Heat the oil in a heavy-based ovenproof frying pan, add the potatoes and fry very gently for 10 minutes, turning frequently, until softened but not browned.

Add the onions and fry gently for a further 5 minutes without browning. Spread the potatoes and onions in an even layer in the pan and turn the heat down as low as possible.

Beat the eggs in a bowl with the herbs and season to taste. Pour the eggs into the pan, cover and cook very gently for about 15 minutes until the eggs have set.

If the centre of the omelette is still liquid, place the pan under a preheated moderate grill to finish cooking. Tip the tortilla on to a plate and serve warm or cold.

WILD MUSHROOM STROGANOFF & SWEET POTATO MASH

The creamy calming mushroom stroganoff is counterbalanced by the antioxidant-rich sweet potatoes.

Preparation time: 15 minutes
Cooking time: 20 minutes
Serves 4
....

25 g (1 oz) **butter**
1 tbsp **olive oil**
1 **onion**, sliced
400 g (13 oz) **chestnut mushrooms**, sliced
2 **garlic cloves**, finely chopped
2 tsps **paprika**, plus extra to garnish
6 tbsps **vodka**
400 ml (14 fl oz) **vegetable stock**
generous pinch of **ground cinnamon**
generous pinch of **ground mace**
150 g (5 oz) **wild mushrooms**, sliced if large
6 tbsps **crème fraîche**
sea salt and **black pepper**
chopped **parsley**, to garnish

Sweet potato mash
3 large **sweet potatoes**, peeled and cubed
2 tbsps **crème fraîche**
1 tsp grated **nutmeg**

Cook the sweet potatoes in a saucepan of lightly salted boiling water for 15–20 minutes, or until tender. Drain, season to taste and mash with the crème fraîche and nutmeg.
....

Meanwhile, heat the butter and oil in a frying pan, add the onion and cook for 5 minutes until lightly browned. Stir in the chestnut mushrooms and garlic and cook for 4 minutes until tender. Stir in the paprika and cook for a further 1 minute.
....

Pour in the vodka. When it is bubbling, flame with a match and stand well back. Once the flames have subsided, stir in the stock, cinnamon and mace and season to taste. Simmer for 3–4 minutes.
....

Add the wild mushrooms and cook for 2 minutes or until tender, then stir in 2 tablespoons of the crème fraîche. Divide between 4 serving plates, top with the remaining crème fraîche and garnish with a sprinkling of paprika and a little parsley. Serve with the sweet potato mash.
....

BAKED SWEET POTATOES WITH VEGETABLE CHILLI

This is an easy, filling dish designed to satisfy and calm. The chilli freezes well and can also be served in warmed corn tortillas.

Preparation time: 20 minutes
Cooking time: about 40 minutes
Serves 4

2 tbsps **olive oil**
1 large **onion**, chopped
400 g (13 oz) **butternut squash**,
    peeled and cubed
1 tsp **cayenne pepper**
1 tsp **ground cumin**
1 tsp **ground cinnamon**
2 **red peppers**, cored, deseeded
    and chopped
1 **courgette**, cubed
1 **red chilli**, deseeded and finely sliced
1 **green chilli**, deseeded and finely sliced
3 **garlic cloves**, finely sliced
400 g (13 oz) can **chickpeas**, rinsed
    and drained
400 g (13 oz) can **red kidney beans**,
    rinsed and drained
2 x 400 g (13 oz) cans chopped **tomatoes**
large bunch of fresh **coriander**
4 **sweet potatoes**, scrubbed
sea salt and **black pepper**
125 ml (4 fl oz) **soured cream**, to serve

Heat the oil in a large saucepan and add the onion. Cook for about 10 minutes over a medium heat until golden and caramelized. Add the squash, cayenne pepper, cumin and cinnamon and season to taste. Cook for 1–2 minutes.

Add the peppers, courgettes, chillies and garlic and cook for another 3–4 minutes. Add the chickpeas, beans and tomatoes and the stalks from the bunch of coriander.

Meanwhile, prick the sweet potatoes all over with a fork and place in a preheated oven, 200°C (400°F), Gas Mark 6, for 20–30 minutes, or until cooked all the way through.

Simmer the chilli, covered, for about 25 minutes until the sauce is thick and the vegetables tender, adding a little water if it becomes too dry. Season to taste, sprinkle with the coriander leaves and serve with the baked sweet potatoes topped with the soured cream.

TURKEY BURGERS WITH SWEET POTATO WEDGES

This is a family-friendly meal for a relaxing evening in. The tryptophan-rich turkey ensures a good night's sleep.

Preparation time: 20 minutes
Cooking time: 30–40 minutes
Serves 4

....

500 g (1 lb) minced **turkey**
2 spring **onions**, finely chopped
2 tsps **dried tarragon**
½ tsp **sea salt**
½ tsp **black pepper**
1 **egg**, lightly beaten
4 **wholemeal buns**
4 large slices of **tomato**
4 **lettuce leaves**

Sweet potato wedges
4 large **sweet potatoes**, peeled
    and cut into wedges
1 tbsp **olive oil**, plus extra for greasing
1 tsp **paprika**
½ tsp **sea salt**
½ tsp **black pepper**

Use your hands to toss together all the ingredients for the sweet potato wedges in a large bowl then arrange on a greased baking sheet. Place on the top shelf of a preheated oven, 200°C (400°F), Gas Mark 6, for 30–40 minutes, or until golden and crisp.

Meanwhile, mix the turkey with the spring onions, tarragon, salt and pepper, then stir in the egg until well combined. Use your hands to shape the mixture into 4 large balls, then press them firmly into burger shapes.

Place under a preheated hot grill for about 8 minutes on each side, or until golden and cooked through. Serve each burger in a wholemeal bun, with a slice of tomato and lettuce, and sweet potato wedges on the side.

HERBY QUINOA WITH LEMON & CHICKEN

Quinoa is rich in omega oils to boost brain power and nourish the nervous system. What's more, it is delicious.

Preparation time: 15 minutes
Cooking time: 15 minutes
Serves 4

200 g (7 oz) **quinoa**
1 tbsp **olive oil**
1 **onion**, chopped
1 **garlic clove**, crushed
500 g (1 lb) **chicken breast fillets**, sliced
1 tsp **ground coriander**
½ tsp **ground cumin**
50 g (2 oz) **dried cranberries**
75 g (3 oz) soft **dried apricots**, chopped
4 tbsps chopped **parsley**
4 tbsps chopped **mint**
finely grated rind of 1 **lemon**
sea salt and **black pepper**

Cook the quinoa in a saucepan of lightly salted boiling water for 15 minutes until tender, then drain.

Meanwhile, heat the oil in a large frying pan, add the onion and cook for 5 minutes until softened. Add the garlic, chicken, coriander and cumin and cook for a further 8–10 minutes until the chicken is cooked through.

Add the chicken mixture, cranberries, apricots, herbs and lemon rind to the quinoa and season to taste. Stir well and serve warm or cold.

CHICKEN & BARLEY RISOTTO

Barley is a wonderfully nutritious grain that works well in this light risotto, offering a good hit of calming B vitamins.

Preparation time: 10 minutes
Cooking time: 40 minutes
Serves 4

900 ml (1½ pints) **chicken stock**
2 tbsps **olive oil**
1 large **onion**, finely chopped
300 g (10 oz) mixed **mushrooms**
2 **garlic cloves**, crushed
200 g (7 oz) **pearl barley**
300 g (10 oz) **asparagus**, trimmed
    and chopped
200 g (7 oz) cooked **chicken**, cubed
50 g (2 oz) **Parmesan cheese**, grated
finely grated rind of 1 **lemon**
sea salt and **black pepper**

Heat the stock in a saucepan until it reaches simmering point, and allow it to continue simmering while you cook.

Heat the olive oil in a large saucepan or frying pan and add the onion. Cook gently for 5–10 minutes until soft, then stir in the mushrooms and garlic. Turn up the heat and cook for 4–5 minutes until tender.

Add the barley and a ladleful of hot stock and cook gently, stirring continuously, until the stock has all but been absorbed. Add another ladleful of stock and repeat until only about 2 ladlefuls of stock remain in the saucepan.

Add the asparagus and chicken to the remaining stock in the saucepan and simmer for 2–3 minutes while you continue to stir the risotto.

Add the remaining stock, asparagus and chicken to the risotto and cook until the barley is tender and all of the liquid has been absorbed. Stir in the Parmesan cheese and lemon rind, season to taste and serve immediately.

LAMB & FLAGEOLET BEAN STEW

Lamb is an excellent source of iron and pulses help sustain energy levels, ensuring you feel full for hours.

Preparation time: 15 minutes
Cooking time: 1 hour 25 minutes
Serves 4

1 tsp **olive oil**
350 g (11½ oz) **lean lamb**, cubed
16 small **shallots**, peeled
1 **garlic clove**, crushed
1 tbsp **plain flour**
600 ml (1 pint) **lamb stock**
200 g (7 oz) can **chopped tomatoes**
1 **bouquet garni**
2 x 400 g (13 oz) cans **flageolet beans**,
    rinsed and drained
250 g (8 oz) **cherry tomatoes**
sea salt and **black pepper**
brown rice or **green beans**, to serve

Heat the oil in a large saucepan over a medium-high heat, add the lamb and cook for 3-4 minutes until browned all over. Remove from the pan and set aside.

Reduce the heat, add the shallots and garlic to the pan and cook gently for 4-5 minutes until softened and just beginning to brown.

Return the lamb and any juices to the pan, stir in the flour and add the stock, tomatoes, bouquet garni and beans. Bring to the boil, stirring, then cover and simmer for 1 hour until the lamb is just tender.

Add the cherry tomatoes and season to taste. Continue to simmer for 10 minutes, then serve with brown rice or green beans.

MANGO BRÛLÉE

This delicious, warming dessert provides a host of key nutrients, including yogurt to calm and encourage healthy digestion.

Preparation time: 10 minutes
Cooking time: 5 minutes
Serves 4

2 large, ripe **mangoes**, peeled, stoned and sliced
2 tsps **rum** or 2 tsps **vanilla extract**
1 tsp **ground cinnamon**
350 ml (12 fl oz) **live Greek yogurt**
6 tsps **brown sugar**

Divide the sliced mango between 4 small ovenproof dishes, filling them about half way, then drizzle with the rum or vanilla, and sprinkle with the cinnamon.

Spoon the yogurt over the mango and smooth to level. Sprinkle with the brown sugar then place under a preheated medium grill for about 5 minutes, until the sugar begins to bubble and caramelize. Serve immediately.

BLUEBERRY & LEMON ICE CREAM

Blueberries help balance weight and ease anxiety. This refreshing ice cream can be enjoyed any time.

Preparation time: 10 minutes, plus freezing
Serves 4
....

500 g (1 lb) **frozen blueberries**
500 ml (17 fl oz) **live Greek yogurt**
125 g (4 oz) **icing sugar**,
    plus extra to decorate
finely grated rind and juice of 2 **lemons**

Set aside a few blueberries for decoration. Place the remaining blueberries in a blender or food processor with the yogurt, icing sugar and lemon rind and juice and blend until smooth.

....

Spoon the mixture into a 600 ml (1 pint) freezerproof container and freeze until softly frozen and easily spoonable. Before serving, decorate with the reserved blueberries and a sprinkling of icing sugar.

....

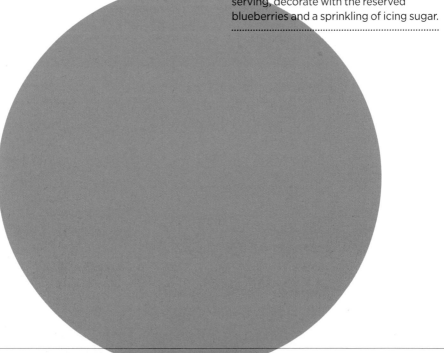

BAKED BANANAS

Bananas contain multiple stress-busting nutrients so this delicious dessert is the perfect way to end a stressful day.

Preparation time: 15 minutes
Cooking time: 20 minutes
Serves 4

....

4 large firm **bananas**
2 tsps **brown sugar**
1 tsp **vanilla extract**
1 tsp **maple syrup**
1½ tsps **butter**
handful of **almonds**
    or **pistachios**, chopped (optional)
live Greek yogurt, to serve

Make a long slit down the centre of each of the unpeeled bananas. Place each banana, cut-side up, in the centre of a large piece of foil.

....

Mix together sugar, vanilla, maple syrup and butter, and spoon into the slits in the bananas. Wrap carefully in the foil, ensuring that the bananas remain upright with the slits at the top.

....

Place in a preheated oven, 200°C (400°F), Gas Mark 6, for 20 minutes. Open the parcels, sprinkle with the nuts, if using, and serve immediately with Greek yogurt.

....

BROWN RICE PUDDING

Brown rice gives this creamy pudding a nutty flavour and a hit of stress-busting nutrients.

Preparation time: 10 minutes
Cooking time: about 1¾ hours
Serves 4
....

325 ml (11 fl oz) **double cream**, oat cream
   or soya cream
300 ml (½ pint) **water**
100 g (3½ oz) **brown rice**
75 g (3 oz) **sultanas, raisins**
   or **dried cranberries**
3 **egg yolks**
3 tsps **demerara sugar**
1 tsp **ground cinnamon**
2 tsps **vanilla extract**
1 tsp **butter**, melted

Place the cream, measurement water and rice in a large, heavy-based saucepan over a medium heat and stir well. Bring to the boil, then reduce the heat to a simmer and cook for about 1½ hours, stirring regularly, until the rice is tender and all of the liquid has been absorbed. Add a little more water if it starts to dry out.

....

Stir in the dried fruit and cook for a further 10 minutes until plump, stirring frequently.

....

Mix the egg yolks, sugar, cinnamon, vanilla and butter in a small bowl, then add to the rice mixture and cook over a gentle heat for about 5 minutes, stirring constantly, until it thickens. Remove from the heat and serve immediately.

....

CRANBERRY & APPLE CRUMBLE

This is a great winter warmer with a crunchy, nutty topping, rich in healthy oils and soothing oats.

Preparation time: 20 minutes
Cooking time: 30 minutes
Serves 4
....

4 **cooking apples**, peeled,
    cored   and finely sliced
2 tsps **cornflour**
2 tsps **ground cinnamon**
4 tsps **honey**
100 g (3½ oz) **fresh** or **dried cranberries**
finely grated rind and juice of 1 **orange**
live Greek yogurt, to serve

Topping
200 g (7 oz) **porridge oats**
2 tsps **ground cinnamon**
50 g (2 oz) **almonds**, crushed
50 g (2 oz) **brazil nuts**, crushed
2 drops of **vanilla extract**
2 tsps **butter**, melted, plus extra for dotting

Place the apples in a large bowl and stir in the cornflour, cinnamon, honey and cranberries until coated, and then add the orange juice and rind. Transfer the mixture to an ovenproof dish and press down lightly.

Mix together all the topping ingredients, then press on top of the apple and cranberry mixture and dot with a little extra butter.

Place in a preheated oven, 200°C (400°F), Gas Mark 6, for 30 minutes, or until the topping is golden and the apple juices are starting to bubble up at the edges of the dish. Serve hot with yogurt.

CHERRY & CINNAMON PARFAIT

Cinnamon boosts immunity, stabilizes blood sugar, encourages brain function and reduces levels of cortisol.

Preparation time: 10 minutes, plus cooling and freezing
Cooking time: 5 minutes
Serves 4

350 g (11½ oz) jar **Morello cherries** in syrup
3 tsps **ground cinnamon**
1 tsp **vanilla extract**
1 tsp **caster sugar**
1 **egg yolk**
150 g (5 oz) **half-fat crème fraîche**
4 **meringue nests**, broken into pieces
fresh cherries, to decorate

Drain the cherries and measure 100 ml (3½ fl oz) of the syrup into a small saucepan. Stir in the cinnamon, vanilla and sugar and heat for 5 minutes or until the sugar has dissolved. Set aside to cool.

Mix the egg yolk and crème fraîche. Add the drained cherries to the syrup, then stir in the crème fraîche and egg. Fold the crushed meringue carefully through the mixture.

Transfer to a 300 ml (½ pint) freezerproof container and freeze for at least 4 hours. Eat within a day, when the parfait will be softly frozen. Decorate with fresh cherries before serving.

RICOTTA, PLUM & ALMOND CAKE

Plums and almonds are a wonderful combination. This nutritious cake makes a lovely dessert or snack, rich in omega oils.

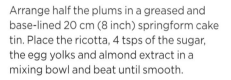

Preparation time: 20 minutes, plus cooling and chilling
Cooking time: 35 minutes
Serves 6

....

butter, for greasing
500 g (1 lb) **sweet red plums**, quartered and stoned
250 g (8 oz) **ricotta cheese**
4–5 tsps light soft **brown sugar**
3 **eggs**, separated
¼ tsp **almond extract**
4 tsps **flaked almonds**
2 tsps **water**
1 tsp **icing sugar**, sifted, to serve

Arrange half the plums in a greased and base-lined 20 cm (8 inch) springform cake tin. Place the ricotta, 4 tsps of the sugar, the egg yolks and almond extract in a mixing bowl and beat until smooth.

Whisk the egg whites in a clean bowl until stiff peaks form. Carefully fold into the ricotta mixture, then spoon over the plums.

Sprinkle the top with the flaked almonds and place in a preheated oven, 160°C (325°F), Gas Mark 3, for 30–35 minutes until the cake is well risen, golden brown and the centre is just set. Cover the top loosely with foil after 20 minutes if it is browning too quickly.

Turn off the oven and leave the cake to cool for 15 minutes with the door slightly ajar. Cool completely, then chill in the refrigerator.

Meanwhile, cook the remaining plums with the measurement water in a covered saucepan for 5 minutes. Remove from the heat, cool slightly, then in a blender or food processor blend until smooth. Taste and add the remaining sugar if necessary.

Transfer the cake to a serving plate. Dust the top with the icing sugar and serve, cut into wedges, with the plum sauce.

BLUEBERRY FOOL

You'll get a big hit of antioxidant-rich blueberries in this creamy dessert, which takes only minutes to make.

Preparation time: 5 minutes
Serves 4
....

400 g (13 oz) **blueberries**
5 tsps **honey**
2 tsps **lime juice**
8 **mint leaves**
125 ml (4 fl oz) ready-made **low-fat custard**
250 ml (8 fl oz) **live Greek yogurt**
4 tsps finely chopped unsalted **pistachios**

Place the blueberries, honey, lime juice and half the mint leaves in a blender or food processor and blend until smooth.
....

Add the custard and yogurt and blend again to combine. Spoon into individual glasses, sprinkle with the pistachios and top with the remaining mint leaves before serving.
....

RASPBERRY YOGURT GRATIN

Bursting with antioxidants and digestion-boosting live yogurt, this is a delicious dessert with surprisingly few calories.

Preparation time: 5 minutes, plus cooling
Cooking time: 5-6 minutes
Serves 4
....

500 g (1 lb) **raspberries**
350 ml (12 fl oz) **live Greek yogurt**
2 tsps **vanilla extract**
1 tsp **cassis** or **blackcurrant cordial**
2 tsps light soft **brown sugar**

Place the raspberries in a shallow ovenproof dish. Beat the yogurt with the vanilla and cassis or cordial, then spoon over the raspberries and level the surface.
....

Sprinkle the brown sugar evenly over the top, then place under a preheated hot grill for 5-6 minutes until the sugar starts to caramelize. Cool slightly then serve.
....

DARK CHOCOLATE FONDUE WITH FRUIT & NUTS

This is a decadent, mood-boosting treat, which is elegant enough to serve at a dinner party.

Preparation time: 5 minutes
Cooking time: 10 minutes
Serves 4

················

100 g (3½ oz) **dark chocolate**
1 tsp **salted butter**
1 tsp **vanilla extract**
2 tsps **live natural yogurt**

To dip
brazil nuts
almonds
dried apricots
grapes
cherries

Melt the chocolate in a heatproof bowl over a saucepan of gently simmering water, making sure the water does not touch the bottom of the bowl. Stir until melted and shiny.

·····························

Add the butter, vanilla and yogurt and stir until well combined. Remove from the heat and serve immediately, with the nuts and fruit for dipping.

··

SOUR CHERRY CHOCOLATE BROWNIE PUDDING

Sour cherries, which provide a host of emotional and physical benefits, are teamed here with sweet, rich chocolate.

Preparation time: 15 minutes
Cooking time: 15 minutes
Serves 4

....

75 g (3 oz) **unsalted butter**, softened, plus extra for greasing
100 g (3½ oz) light soft **brown sugar**
1 tsp **vanilla extract**
25 g (1 oz) **cocoa powder**, sifted
50 g (2 oz) **self-raising flour**, sifted
1 **egg**
50 g (2 oz) **dried sour cherries**
double cream or **crème fraîche**, to serve

Place the butter, sugar and vanilla in a bowl and beat with a hand-held electric whisk until light and fluffy. Add the cocoa, flour and egg and whisk until combined, then stir in the cherries.

....

Spoon the mixture into 4 holes of a lightly greased 6-hole nonstick muffin tin and place in a preheated oven, 180°C (350°F), Gas Mark 4, for 10–12 minutes or until just cooked but still soft in the centres.

....

Turn out the puddings on to 4 serving plates and serve immediately with double cream or crème fraîche.

....

RESOURCES

Anxiety UK
Tel: 0161 227 9898
Email: info@anxietyuk.org.uk
Website: www.anxietyuk.org.uk

**British Association for Counselling and
Psychotherapy**
Tel: 0870 443 5252
Email: bacp@bacp.co.uk
Website: www.bacp.co.uk

British Heart Foundation
Helpline: 020 7935 0185
Website: www.bhf.org.uk

British Meditation Society
Tel: 01460 62921
Website: www.britishmeditationsociety.org

British Nutrition Foundation
Tel: 020 7557 7930
Email: postbox@nutrition.org.uk
Website: www.nutrition.org.uk

British Wheel of Yoga
Tel: 01529 306 851
Website: www.bwy.org.uk

Channel 4: Stress Magazine
Website: www.channel4.com/health/microsites/H/
health/magazine/stress/home_main.html

MIND
Tel: 0845 766 1063
Email: contact@mind.org.uk
Website: www.mind.org.uk
National Stress Awareness Day
Email: nsad@isma.org.uk
Website: www.nsad.org.uk

The Nutrition Society
Tel: 020 7602 0228
Email: office@nutsoc.org.uk
Website: www.nutsoc.org.uk

Patient.co.uk
Relaxation Exercises
Website: http://www.patient.co.uk/health/
Relaxation-Exercises.htm

Samaritans
UK helpline: 08457 909090
Email: jo@samaritans.org
Website: www.samaritans.org.uk

Sane
Helpline: 0845 767 8000
Email: info@sane.org.uk
Website: www.sane.org.uk

Stress Management Society
Tel: 08701 999 235
Email: info@stress.org.uk
Website: www.stress.org.uk

INDEX

Acknowledgements

Gill Paul would like to
thank the very talented
team at Octopus: Denise
Bates, who came up
with the idea for the
series; Katy Denny, Alex
Stetter and Jo Wilson
who edited the books so
efficiently and made it
all work; and to the
design team of Jonathan
Christie and Isabel de
Cordova for making it all
look so gorgeous. Thank
you also to Karel Bata
for all the support and
for eating my cooking.

Karen Sullivan would
like to thank Cole, Luke
and Marcus.

Picture credits

Commissioned
photography ©
Octopus Publishing
Group/Will Heap
apart from the
following:
Alamy: Roderick
Chen 16.
Octopus Publishing
Group: Will Heap 125;
Emma Neish 65; Lis
Parsons 37, 71, 81, 85,
111, 117; William Shaw
49, 67, 87, 93, 99,
107, 119.
Thinkstock: iStock-
photo 5, 7, 8, 9, 10, 12,
25, 27, 28, 34.